SELLING CRAFTS

Robert S. L. Nathan set up his own business as a self-employed toymaker in 1980, initially making educational toys for the under-5s, then miniature metal toys for dolls' houses, many of which are now sold in the export markets. He was chairman of the British Toymakers Guild for three years and is presently a member of the Toy Safety Committee of the British Standards Institution.

SELLING CRAFTS

Robert S. L. Nathan

David & Charles
Newton Abbot   London   North Pomfret (Vt)

To
Florence Syu Li
Without whose help and moral support I would
never have found the courage to become a
self-employed craftsman

Every effort has been made to ensure that
the information given in this book is accurate, but
no responsibility can be accepted for any errors
or omissions

British Library Cataloguing in Publication Data
Nathan, Robert S. L.
Selling crafts.
1. Handicrafts – Marketing
I. Title
745.5'068'8   HD2341

ISBN 0–7153–8803–7

Photoset by
Northern Phototypesetting Co Bolton
and printed in Great Britain
by A. Wheaton & Co Ltd Exeter
for David & Charles Publishers plc
Brunel House Newton Abbot Devon

Published in the United States of America
by David & Charles Inc
North Pomfret Vermont 05053 USA

Contents

Introduction

Most of the books that have been published on the subject of starting up in business have been written by accountants, lecturers or civil servants. Should you decide you too want to treat this as a theoretical subject, they will be well worth the effort of reading.

This book, imperfect as it may be, has been written by a full-time, 'paint-in-the-moustache' craftsman. Its information has been culled from personal experiences, both my own and those of other craftspeople in small businesses, and it should highlight some of the treats and traps that lie in wait for the unsuspecting craftsperson.

In order to start up a craft business, you do not require vast sums of cash; indeed, it can sometimes be a distinct disadvantage to be over-capitalised. Nor do you need a well-equipped workshop. All you really need is the germ of an idea, faith in yourself, unlimited optimism, encouragement from friends and family and, most important of all, no alternative.

Hard as it may be, try not to be over-influenced by people who offer you advice. Always remember that it will be you, in the final analysis, who has to accept the consequences of any decision you make. And when the 'mucky stuff hits the punkah' you needn't bother to look for your advisers.

To my mind one of the finest things about being a self-employed craftsman is the independence. If self-discipline is not one of your faults, you are going to have a few initial problems. You will have to learn very quickly how to structure your day but once you have come to terms with the shock of having to rely on your own wit and low cunning in order to survive, you should be ready to get the most out of being a self-employed craftsperson.

I sincerely hope that I shall succeed in getting across the message that making and selling crafts can be a great deal of fun. If you have enough determination and faith in yourself, it will offer you an incredibly satisfying way of earning your living.

R.S.L.N.
London

I
STARTING A CRAFT
BUSINESS

1
From Home-made to Hand-made

One of the first things to be taken into account, when you make the momentous decision to put yourself and your product at the mercy of the craft-buying public, is the great and often indefinable distinction between an item that is (or appears to be) home-made and one that is hand-made.

For the purposes of this book, the definition of home-made is something that, whilst not necessarily made at home (although it usually is), tends to be made from inferior materials, is poorly finished and is as a rule not of merchantable quality. While hand-made items, which *are* more often than not made at home, possess all the attendant virtues of craftsmanship, and display that certain professionalism of attitude and self-assuredness that is the mark of the potentially successful craftsperson.

Because of the difficulties inherent in objective self-criticism, this qualitative distinction may not be instantly recognisable to you with regard to your own workmanship, but I am certain that you will be able to detect it without too much difficulty in other people's work. It is that intangible quality that distinguishes a good craft item from the rest.

People wiser than I have fought shy of defining what constitutes a 'good' product or a 'real' craft. I wouldn't trust anybody who could dictate such rules. There is no trick or easy solution to quality craftsmanship, but I subscribe to the view that a product should be both aesthetically pleasing and suited to its particular purpose (ie functional).

One of the principal joys of being involved in crafts is the individualistic attitude of each craftsperson to his or her work. Nevertheless, the success of whatever you decide to make will in all probability depend, to a greater or lesser extent, on part or all of the following criteria:

- Originality of design and/or interpretation of a traditional design
- Suitability of materials for end-use
- Quality of manufacture and finish
- Suitability of design for end-use
- Aesthetic value
- Value for money

In my experience, most craftspeople who have successfully taken the decision that you are contemplating have, whether by design or default, attained if not all these criteria, then at least one of them. If it is any consolation, it doesn't really matter which one, so long as you think you have an innate capability constantly to learn and improve. It is a salutary lesson to compare the work you are producing this year with the quality of previous years, and so it should continue for as long as you are active in crafts.

This brings us onto the delicate subject of the buying public, for it is they who will finally decide whether you will succeed in your chosen career as a craftsperson – or even have three square meals a day.

Don't be afraid of the public. They do not bite (well, not very often), and whereas you will find the odd one or two who will try to denigrate or diminish your skills, there are just as many, if not more, who will gladly buy your work and behave as though their very existence was made whole by possessing an item created by you. Similarly, don't be afraid of trying out your product on the public. Let them do your market research for you in the most practical way possible: they will either buy your work or not. At the end of a day at a craft market or similar event you will have heard a multitude of reasons, usually conflicting, for the success or failure of your work, added to which of course you may have earned some money by having sold your work.

11

The next step, once you have decided you want to earn your living by making and selling crafts, is rather more mundane. I appreciate that the mere mention of banks, accountants and lawyers may be enough to set your digestive juices churning, but it will not do any harm to discuss them at this early stage and to put them into their proper perspective, in how they will affect you when you start to put yourself on a proper business footing.

The longer one stays in business, the more important and useful one's chosen adviser becomes. However, I lay down one golden rule: Remember, whatever you may be told to the contrary, that you and your customers are the most important people involved in your business. Your advisers are important only so long as they remain useful in furthering and consolidating your interests. This may sound awfully pompous, but I have heard too many times of craftspeople being talked down to by those who wouldn't know a creative thought process if it bit them on their pin-striped leg. Therefore, whilst I would urge you to approach business experts and to heed their advice, never forget that lawyers and financial advisers are in the context of your business merely tools that help you improve your efficiency, and expensive tools at that; so when the time comes to consult them, use them cost-effectively.

2
The Unholy Trinity: Your Professional Advisers

Once you have made the decision to start up in business, you will make contact with the professional advisers whom I have perhaps unkindly called 'the unholy trinity'. Whether you intend to be a small company working out of your spare room, or a tyro tycoon, it will certainly be in your best interest to have the goodwill and expertise of bank managers, accountants and solicitors working for you – rather than against you, should you choose to ignore them.

Unless your family had the foresight to provide you with a pool of relatives well placed in finance and the law, you will soon realise that 'nothing is for nothing'. Don't be embarrassed to shop around, because, regardless of the fact that your advisers are professionals of unquestioned probity, they are no different from you, in that they too are selling a commodity. The only real difference is that they are probably better at selling what they have to offer than are most craftspeople.

CHOOSING YOUR ADVISERS

THE BANK MANAGER
This is intended to be more of a guideline than a hard and fast rule. Take this opportunity to consider what sort of adviser will be most suited to your purposes, and also your pocket. In the case of your bank manager, regardless of which of the 'Big Five' you intend to honour with your overdraft (more of that later),

give some thought to the options that are open to you:

● A suburban branch which deals predominantly with private customers and their associated household finances, but will not be geared up to deal with the special requirements of a business, no matter how small.

● A large city branch which is used to dealing with large businesses and intricate financial wheeling and dealing but which will, with some justification, put you and your company rather low on its list of priorities.

● A bank that is situated near enough to you to be easily accessible and is surrounded by shops or small businesses is most likely to offer you the best service. The staff will be aware of the funny little ways that craftspeople are prone to (like holding up the queue whilst they pay in bags full of coppers) and the manager will understand and, perhaps, be sympathetic towards the peculiar requirements of the small small-businessperson.

Bear in mind, however, that, regardless of what the advertising campaigns may state, a bank is only as good as its local branch manager, who is given far greater autonomy to make decisions on your behalf than you may at first be aware of.

Before you go to see your prospective bank manager, prepare a realistic guesstimate (halfway between a guess and an estimate) of how you anticipate your business will perform in its first and second years. You will be under no obligation to keep to these figures, but if they are within the bounds of reality they will impress upon the bank manager the fact that you have at least given careful thought to your project and that it is not just a wild scheme that will leave everyone's face with an egg-coating. It will also be an interesting exercise for you to see whether or not your plans are viable, how much you will need to earn in order to pay the rent, suppliers etc, to say nothing of your own wages (see 'Raising Capital' page 32).

Bear in mind what I said about the amount of independence branch managers are allowed to exercise and do not hesitate to ask as many questions as you like before committing yourself to opening an account at a specific branch. Feel free to shop around for the best deal that is offered to you; and should you decide at some later date that your bank is not giving you the support or service you had hoped for, make an appointment to see the manager (I have rarely heard of anybody seeing a manager without an appointment) and discuss your problem whilst it is still at an early stage.

If you are still not satisfied, your ultimate sanction will be to remove your account, either to another branch of the same bank or to an entirely different bank. You can do this with complete impunity. It is strange how many people, believing unquestioningly in the 'professions', are under the delusion that moving a bank account is tantamount to denying the 'True Faith': it is nothing of the kind. However, your case will be considerably weakened if in the bank's estimation you are a poor financial risk or are heavily overdrawn. By dint of careful presentation and persuasion it *is* possible for your overdraft and other commitments to be transferred to a new account from your old bank, but before doing so you should consider your position very carefully.

If you regard banks as suppliers of a service for which you pay, you will not find it so hard to consider them as you would any of your other suppliers. The only real difference is that the banks have formed a virtual cartel and maintain a strict monopoly that would be unacceptable in any other field of commerce.

It is highly likely that the bank manager will coyly mention the magic word 'overdraft' when you go to see him. Whilst it will be helpful for you to negotiate an overdraft facility, in case the need for one should ever arise, bear in mind that banks are not philanthropic organisations. Their profits are derived from interest paid to them on overdrafts, and judging by their annual profits they are undoubtedly much better at earning money than you or I. In other words, don't be gulled into believing that the tooth-fairy sits behind a desk wearing a pin-stripe suit. As far as the bank is concerned, its largesse is very 'big bucks'.

If you can avoid going into debt from your first day's trading, it will be to your advantage. Then, afterwards, when you have built up a track record with your bank, you will be able to use your overdraft facility to cope with unexpected outlays (for those sudden large orders that I hope you will receive) or to expand your business.

As a 'business' account you will be treated quite differently from 'personal' accounts, in that you will, in all probability, be asked to pay bank charges regardless of whether you are in credit or not.

You will find that this is the major variation between the large banking organisations, and it may be the deciding factor in your choice of bank for your new business. Some banks will charge you for each cheque drawn on your account. Others will charge you a percentage of cash turnover on your account. The most annoying practice is when you are also charged for paying cash *into* your account – the rule of at least one of the major banks, because of its practice of levying a charge on every individual counter transaction, whether it be a withdrawal or a payment.

Your bank manager's discretionary powers will also apply to the levying of bank charges, so why not ask him to waive them for the first few quarters? You might suggest that it would be a positive and constructive way of encouraging a small business. It does sometimes work, and it will certainly save you a few pounds at the outset of your career when you need it most.

It is in your best interest to try to keep your business and private bank accounts separate, even though it may sometimes be hard to tell the difference. If you start as you mean to continue, it will certainly save you from all kinds of embarrassment when some nosy chap from the 'Revenue' starts trying to make sense of your account books.

THE ACCOUNTANT

When choosing a suitable accountant consider the alternatives that we have already discussed with regard to your choice of bank manager: that is, try to find an individual or firm who will understand your particular circumstances as a small business.

One of the most reliable methods of making your choice is from the personal recommendation of other craftspeople, who have probably at some time been in the same position that you find yourself in now.

Make certain that whomever you choose is a *qualified* accountant. They will have FCA or ACA after their name. If your accounts are to be taken seriously by the tax authorities, they should be checked at year-end by a qualified accountant, not by a book-keeper with delusions of grandeur.

Although only limited companies are legally obliged to keep up-to-date records of accounts, it is an extremely good discipline for you to keep accounts, even if initially they are fairly rudimentary. Then, when the Tax Man catches up with you, as he undoubtedly will, it will actually cost you less in time, trouble and cash to be able to supply him with a set of audited accounts. The most basic set of 'books' that you should keep for your business are listings of:

● Sales – invoices for goods that you have supplied.
● Purchases – invoices for goods that you have purchased.
● Cheques – copied from your business account chequebook.
● Paying-in-book – copied from your business account paying-in-book.

Added to this, you must keep all the sales invoices, purchase invoices, cheque stubs, paying-in books and any other relevant paperwork for at least six years so that your entries can be verified at a later date.

Your accountant will undoubtedly advise you in considerably greater detail how to maintain your books so that they can be audited with the least possible waste of time. As you will be charged by the hour for the services of an accountant, this is definitely worth remembering. Similarly it will be entirely up to you whether you maintain and update your own books and simply give them to your accountant for an end-of-year audit and balance or let your accountant do everything for you, which to my mind is a needless expense.

Regardless of how you keep your books, you should find that a conscientious accountant will take the trouble to visit you a couple of times at least in the early months of your business, to ensure that you are coping with the paperwork and not making too many mistakes.

When you are in a position to use an accountant, it will free you from the bothersome chores of filling in tax returns and balancing your books for audits. You will then be allowed to carry on the more important job of producing your craft.

THE SOLICITOR

You will be unlikely to require the services of a solicitor very often, which is just as well because they are usually very expensive people to talk to.

Don't, however, let that deter you from contacting one should you feel you need expert advice regarding a potential problem or a legal matter. A short visit to a solicitor early on may, in the long run, save you a lot of money and trouble. Much of the specialised help that you will get from a solicitor may also be obtained free of charge (or for a nominal sum) from some of the trade-development organisations and small business advice centres that exist for this very purpose (see 'Who Can Help You' page 45).

However, should you decide to enter into a partnership or any similar sort of agreement, you *must*, for your own good, tie up all the legal loose ends. In those circumstances a visit to a solicitor who specialises in these matters would be well advised.

Try not to use any of your advisers merely as a crutch, but make your own decisions whenever possible. If you are forever on the phone to them, they will charge you by the minute, and that won't do you any good. Use your common sense about contacting them, only doing so if you cannot obtain sufficiently qualified advice elsewhere.

3
Business Structures

Following your initial decision to set yourself up as a self-employed craftsperson, you will have to make some far-reaching commitments with regard to the legal status of your business.

If you take some time at an early stage of your planning to consider all the options and their possible implications, it could save you a lot of anxiety in the months or even years ahead. A planned business is like possessing an umbrella: if you have it, the chances are that it will not rain, but if you leave your brolly at home, you can be certain it will pour down. Similarly, the only way to ensure that routine day-to-day crises don't erupt into catastrophes is for you to try to be aware of the worst eventuality that might arise and to the best of your ability make contingency plans against its ever happening.

In this chapter we shall examine the advantages and disadvantages of the four alternatives that are most commonly used in the formation of small businesses. Each type of business structure has its own financial implications, and to a certain extent there are legal considerations that you must be aware of. Therefore, before you make your decision, consult an accountant and a solicitor, or at the very least someone who is qualified to advise you in these matters.

SOLE TRADER
The easiest way for you to start up in business is to become a sole trader. You are not legally required to register the formation of this type of business, and you need keep only a rudimentary set of accounts for the Inland Revenue.

In theory, and often in practice, the sole trader is in total control of the business, and in a small business set-up it is very much a case of being an 'owner-driver'.

While sole traders are expected to make all the decisions in the running of the business, they are also held totally accountable for those decisions. For example, though you will benefit from the profits that the business earns, you will also be personally liable for all the debts of the business. This means that your creditors will be entitled to seize not only the assets of the business but also your personal assets and possessions (house, furniture, car, etc) in order to recoup what they are owed.

When you become self-employed you must inform the DHSS and your local Inspector of Taxes regarding your change of employment status within a few days of starting your new business. You should be able to find their addresses and telephone numbers in your local telephone directory under, respectively, Inland Revenue and Department of Health & Social Security. You will have become responsible for paying your own National Insurance contributions and the Income Tax on the profits arising out of the business. For this, however, you should seek guidance from your accountant. Many craftspeople who start their business as sole traders become limited companies after a few years. This usually happens after they have built up a track-record of creditworthiness, and when they reach a point at which their scale of business and credit commitments dictate that they should safeguard their personal wealth against the possibility of creditors' claims.

PARTNERSHIP

By definition a partnership is a business which has two or more proprietors. Since all partners in a firm not only share the profits but are also responsible equally for all the partnership's debts and liabilities, you must be certain of the people whom you are proposing to have as partners. One could compare a business partnership with a marriage, and, as in marriage, a partnership can end up in bitterness and recriminations. Therefore you must set down in black and white at the outset the terms and conditions of the partnership. The salient points that you should consider are:

- Who are the partners?
- The proposed role of each partner in the running of the business (production, finance, design, selling, etc).
- The amount of capital to be introduced by each partner.
- The manner in which decisions are to be taken (equal voting rights?).
- The apportioning of profits.
- How to dissolve the partnership, and how to divide the assets.
- How to release or remove a partner.
- How to admit a new partner.
- The arrangements concerning the share valuation of a partner who retires or dies.
- The management of the firm's bank account and general finances.

You should also agree that the partners take out life assurance, so that the death or disability of one partner does not jeopardise the livelihood of the others.

Consider and discuss all the above points, and any others that may apply to your particular circumstances. Then go to a solicitor and have an agreement drawn up that is acceptable for all parties to sign. By so doing you will be saving all concerned a great deal of trouble in the future, when the first euphoric joy of the partnership will long since have been dissipated by the realities of business.

If you are seriously thinking in terms of teaming up with a partner, analyse your own motives for wanting to do so, and give a lot of thought to the possible advantages and disadvantages that a partnership will offer compared with alternative arrangements. For example, you would undoubtedly find it cost-effective for two or more people to share the expenses of running a business. You would be able to share the responsibility for decision-making (and to blame someone else for mistakes). A partner might also provide valuable expertise, specialised knowledge or simply lots of money. All reasons why people go into partnership together. But do not make the mistake of allowing personal friendship to overcome sound business judgement in choosing a partner; remember, whilst it is essential to enjoy a good working relationship, you will also be mutually dependent on each other for your livelihoods.

The major disadvantage of a partnership is that all the partners are equally responsible for the liabilities of the business, including the payment of taxes, so if one or more of the partners fails to pay up their share, for whatever reason, the debt has to be met by the remaining partners.

There are, of course, numerous successful partnerships but when you consider that craftspeople are, by their nature, individualists, you would be wise to take precautions.

Provided you don't harbour any false illusions about each other and are basically honest, there is no reason to suppose that a partnership will not last forever.

LIMITED COMPANY

A limited company is a much more regulated business structure than the previous options discussed. It is subject to stricter control, and it will involve you in considerably more form-filling and book-keeping, not to mention the preparation of detailed accounts that you are obliged by law to maintain, incurring, as they will, increased accountants' fees.

Unless prevented for professional or legal reasons (if you are an undischarged bankrupt for example), anyone may form or be a director of a limited company. However, because of the taxation, financial and legal implications, you would be well advised to seek advice from your accountant, bank manager and solicitor before you proceed.

The immediate benefit from trading as a limited company is

the protection of limited liability. This means that the liabilities (ie debts) that are incurred by a company are limited to the assets (ie property and money) of that company and that the directors cannot lose more than they have invested as share capital. In the event of your company being bankrupted, the creditors can seize only the company's assets to meet their claims, and your personal property and wealth cannot be touched – assuming, of course, that you haven't been trading fraudulently. In practice, however, you will find that you may be asked to make a personal guarantee for a debt or loan, which will put you back to where you started.

Don't incorporate your business (ie become a limited company) solely for prestige. Those who matter won't take you any less seriously as a businessperson if you do not have 'Ltd' after your trade name, and there is nothing to prevent your including the word 'company' in your business name, even if you are a sole trader or a partnership (NB: you cannot put 'limited').

An incorporated company is subject to the provisions of the Companies Acts. The directors of a company may become personally liable for failure to comply with the requirements of the Acts, ignorance of the law being neither an excuse nor a defence.

The cost of forming a limited company will probably be in the region of £100. You can have one tailor-made to meet the exact requirements of your business (including choice of name) or you can buy a ready-made 'off-the-shelf' company from a firm that specialises in that field. Although there is nothing to prevent your forming your own limited company, or incorporating an existing business, I would seriously recommend that you let the experts (company registration agents) in collaboration with your solicitor and accountant act on your behalf. Company law can appear deceptively simple to the uninitiated, and if a possible future source of aggravation can be eliminated by getting the job done properly at the outset, I think you will agree it will be money well spent.

WORKERS' CO-OPERATIVE

In theory you might assume that a workers' co-operative is the ideal solution for a craftsperson with limited means who wants to start up in business. The reality is often rather different. To quote the Co-operative Development Agency: '. . . a co-operative is not a "soft option". No one should join a co-operative as a passenger . . .'

In order to succeed in the particular conditions that exist in a co-operative, you will need to have a special kind of temperament. Co-operatives seem to be composed of two basic types of people, one very dominant and the other very biddable. Workers' co-operatives differ from other business structures in that they are owned and controlled by the members, who operate a democratic system of management. Decisions are taken on a 'one member, one vote' principle, members being for the main part the employees or workforce of the co-operative.

Workers' co-operatives have a tendency to be polemical and somewhat idealistic, and a lot of time can be taken up by interminable 'political' wrangling between factions among the members. Regardless of the high ideals and genuine aspirations of the members, or maybe because of them, co-operatives have a distressing habit of dividing into these factions and eventually disintegrating.

On the whole, based on the experiences of craftspeople who have been involved in workers' co-operatives, unless you are very committed to the ideals of co-operatives and are prepared to sacrifice some of your independence a co-op is not for you.

Full information on workers' co-operatives and how to set them up can be obtained from the Co-operative Development Agency, Broadmead House, 21 Panton Street, London SW1Y 4DR (01-839 2988).

If you simply feel the need to work with other craftspeople, you might consider simply sharing a workshop and facilities on a less formalised basis than a co-operative.

BUSINESS NAME

With regard to your choice of business name, as an unincorporated business (sole trader or partnership), if you decide to trade under any name other than your own surname, you must display your name and address (at which documents may be served) on all business letters, orders, invoices, receipts and demands for payment. The same information must be prominently displayed at the premises where your business is transacted, or to where your suppliers and customers have access.

For example, if a Ms Muffet sells curds and whey under her own name, she would not be considered as using a business name; whereas if she was the proprietress of 'Miss Muffet's Curds & Whey Co' or 'Tuffet Curds', she would be subject to the regulations.

You may trade under your own name or, with certain restrictions, under any other name that you choose for your business. The restrictions on your choice of business name are basically to deter people from using a name that is either too similar to an existing business or deliberately misleading. For example, a friend of mine called Mason was at college with a girl called Fortnum: 'What a good idea!' they said. 'Let's have a market stall and sell food.' Needless to say, they were politely but firmly dissuaded from calling their proposed business Fortnum & Mason.

Due to the abolition in 1981 of the Registry of Business Names, you will have to be very careful not to use someone else's name to trade under. In theory, the onus is on you to make a search through local directories and old registers, but in practice, unless you are particularly unlucky or flagrant in your choice of business name, you might as well decide on a name and use it. Most people work on the assumption that if they are small enough no one will notice. Obviously this is not very satisfactory, and one should make every effort to stay within the rules, but in this instance one can do very little because at best the regulations are 'non-regulations' while at worst they are a confused mess. If you do want to make sure that you are not inadvertently using someone else's business name, Business Registry Searches, Greyhound Chambers, Moor Street, Chepstow, Gwent NP6 5DP (02912 70138), will, for a fee, make a search on your behalf.

If you do decide to trade under a business name other than your own, give a lot of thought to the name you choose. It should reflect something about you or your product, so that your customers will be able to identify it with you in their minds.

Nothing could be easier for an unincorporated company than to change its name should the need arise. You simply change it, remembering to alter all your stationery accordingly. It will come as no surprise to learn that the situation with regard to a limited company is entirely different.

Limited companies are obliged to submit their choice of business name to the Registrar of Companies, Companies House, Maindy, Cardiff CF4 3UZ (or for Scotland: Exchequer Chambers, George Street, Edinburgh EH2 3DJ) at the same time sending all documents concerning their incorporation. The registrar then allows the choice of name, subject to its not already being registered or otherwise 'unsuitable'. However, the Secretary of State is able to direct a company to change its name up to a year after incorporation if it is subsequently found to be unacceptable.

Limited companies (strictly speaking, private limited companies) must put the word 'Limited' (or the abbreviation 'Ltd') after their business name. Companies with registered offices in Wales may put 'Cyfyngedig' instead, so long as they state in English on all the company stationery and premises that they have done so. A limited company must put the registered name, the address of the registered office, the registration number and place of registration (England, Wales, Scotland) on all the company stationery (letters, invoices, catalogues etc), though they are not required to include the names of directors. A limited company is also required to display clearly ('paint or affix') its name outside each place of business. As with unincorporated businesses, failure to comply with these regulations is punishable by a fine.

To change the name of a limited company, the directors have to pass a 'special resolution' and send it to the Registrar of Companies (together with a £40 fee) detailing the proposed changes. Provided the new name is allowable, the registrar will insert the new name in the index in place of the old and issue a new certificate of incorporation.

There is a list of specified words for which approval must be sought before you may use them. These are predominantly those that imply status (association, institute, trust etc), nationality (British, international etc) or relate to the royal family. A full list of these words is contained in the statutory instrument of the *Company & Business Names Regulations 1981 and 1982.*

If you have any queries regarding the selection of a business name, you should contact the Small Firms Service (telephone Freefone 2444) for advice.

4
Insurance

Don't even think about saving money by not being insured. One of the single most serious mistakes that people make is to think that disasters will not happen to them. Believe me, they do, and if you are not covered by insurance the results can be devastating.

No matter how small your business is, you are unquestionably going to need insurance in some form or other, because if fire or theft prevents your continuing to work, you and your business could be completely wiped out.

When you are ready to take out insurance, arrange it through an insurance broker. Although a broker earns commission from the insurers, you will not be offered a lower premium by dealing directly with the insurance company itself.

A worthwhile firm of insurance brokers will usually be prepared to tailor insurance cover to meet your individual requirements. They will also offer you several competitive quotations from different companies to choose from. You should then be able to negotiate the most favourable deal from among the different quotes on offer. Some insurance companies offer a package deal specifically designed for small businesses, but I strongly suggest that you read the 'fine print' on this sort of cover very carefully indeed, in case it leaves you unprotected because of your specific requirements.

The best way to find a good insurance broker is by personal recommendation. If you are stuck for advice, you should contact the bank that handles your account. All the major banks have highly efficient insurance-broking services that are available for the use of their clients.

As a result of the ever-rising cost of insurance, it is tempting not to review the value of your insured property annually. This could leave you in the position of being markedly under-insured within a couple of years and it is a false economy that could prove expensive in the event of a claim. Try to ensure that you have adequate cover at all times. Your broker should recommend that the insured values accurately reflect current market replacement costs. Whether or not he reminds you when the annual premiums are due to be paid, it is your responsibility to check that everything is correctly valued and paid for.

Insurance companies have acquired a reputation for not paying out on claims. Strictly speaking this is not founded in fact. If you make an honest claim against a loss that you are properly insured for, you will be paid. If, due to either ignorance or bad advice, you have insufficient cover, you cannot reasonably expect to be compensated fully.

Your insurance requirements will vary, depending on what kind of business you propose to have, but generally speaking you will need to be covered for the following:

PREMISES

As a minimum requirement, make absolutely certain that your premises are covered for fire, theft and damage from the moment you become responsible for them (even if you are not yet in occupation). If you are renting property, it may be a stipulation of the lease or licence, but regardless of whether or not you are legally required to do so, you must protect your own interests by being adequately insured. If you are working from home, you must advise your house insurers of that fact, because it will probably affect the status of your existing insurance for house and contents.

CONTENTS

You must make sure that the contents are adequately insured. This should take into consideration the furniture, equipment and 'fixtures and fittings' that you keep on the premises.

STOCK

Insure your stock, bearing in mind that it will be in the form of materials, part-made goods and finished goods, each having a different value. You will have to make an educated guess as to the value of the stock that you hold at any given time, but if you have any doubts about arriving at a figure, consult your broker, who will advise you.

LOSS OF EARNINGS

As a self-employed craftsperson you owe it to yourself to insure against being unable to earn your living. If you should be taken ill or suffer an injury that prevents you from working, you will still be expected to meet your debts and commitments, to say nothing of earning a wage. You can take out a sickness and personal injury policy to cover this eventuality, and you can add a 'loss of earnings' clause against your being unable to work and the consequential loss of business, due to loss of or damage to your premises, contents and/or stock. Another way of insuring against possible loss of earnings is to extend the cover on your premises, contents and stock to include a 'consequential loss' clause. This again is where your broker is the person to advise you as to how to tailor your policy to suit your particular needs.

EMPLOYERS' LIABILITY

Under the Employers' Liability (Compulsory Insurance) Act 1969 you are legally obliged to take out employers' liability insurance if you employ staff, whether they are part-time or full-time. This will cover you against any claim for personal injury or disease that may have been sustained by an employee in the course of their work. A copy of the insurance certificate must be displayed at the place of work. Failure to comply with these legal requirements can result in heavy fines.

PUBLIC LIABILITY

You will need public liability insurance to cover yourself against injury caused to a member of the public or third party in the course of, or as a result of, your business. A claim may arise from an accident to a customer (perhaps they slipped on a polished floor) whilst on your premises, or they may have suffered disease or injury as a direct result of something purchased from you. You are especially advised to take out public liability cover if you export to the USA, where consumer litigation is rife and claims are astronomical. Public liability cover is normally for about £250,000, though as a result of successful claims (mainly in the United States) you may be advised by your broker to take out higher cover.

VEHICLE INSURANCE

If you have a vehicle that you intend to use, even if only occasionally, for business purposes you must ensure that your insurance cover allows you to do so. For example, if you use your vehicle to deliver or collect goods or to carry samples of merchandise, you must inform the insurance company that you are using your vehicle in the course of your business. Otherwise this may nullify your vehicle's insurance completely, which would make it illegal to drive it.

GOODS IN TRANSIT

Businesses that depend on despatching quantities of goods, by either vehicle or post, should take out insurance to cover goods in transit. This insurance will soon pay for itself by obviating the need to pay the post office individual cover or registration on each packet despatched.

A competent broker should advise you regarding what insurance you and your business will need. Make a point of reading the policy very carefully, especially the 'exclusion clauses' and the 'fine print'. If you have any query at all, ask for clarification *before* you agree to take the insurance, rather than find out too late that you have insufficient cover.

5
Raising Capital

In order to start up in business, whether it be making and selling crafts or anything else, sheer talent is not enough. You are going to need money.

Regardless of what you may have thought to the contrary, you do not need a small fortune to start up in business. It is possible to start with £100 or less, and whereas there is no great merit in being under-capitalised, by virtue of careful money management (miserliness by another name), you can start to run a small business on next to nothing. I should stress, however, that by doing so you are left no room for mistakes. So unless you are fairly confident or have no alternative, you should consider arranging some kind of financial safety net for your project.

Most businesses borrow money from the bank, or at the very least have an overdraft facility agreed with their bank manager against the day when they will need to borrow. The time to approach your bank manager with regard to the financial services he can offer you is when your plans are beginning to take definite shape. At this stage you should prepare a serious presentation of your scheme. You may require some assistance in turning your aspirations into a compelling commercial argument for financial backing, in which case you should seek help from one or more of the organisations that offer precisely this kind of expertise (see chapter 7).

If this is your first independent business venture, you will not be able to provide a track record of commercial achievement to prove you are a good financial risk. This will put you at a slight disadvantage, and much will depend on the impression your presentation creates in the mind of the bank manager.

CASHFLOW FORECAST	JAN	FEB	MAR	APR	MAY	JUN	JUL	AUG	SEP	OCT	NOV	DEC	TOTAL
INCOME													
SALES	300	800	900	800	950	850	1400	650	980	1300	1600	1800	12330
OTHERS (GRANTS ETC.)	–	–	–	–	150	–	–	–	–	–	–	–	150
TOTAL CASH REC'D	300	800	900	800	1100	850	1400	650	980	1300	1600	1800	12480
EXPENDITURE													
RENT	100	100	100	100	100	100	100	100	100	100	100	100	1200
RATES	30	–	–	30	30	30	30	30	30	30	30	30	300
FAIRS	–	–	75	–	35	120	60	50	–	150	–	60	550
ELECTRICITY	–	–	40	–	–	15	–	–	20	–	–	25	100
INSURANCE	–	–	–	–	–	–	–	–	140	–	–	–	140
PROFESSIONAL FEES	–	–	–	–	–	–	–	–	120	–	–	–	120
VEHICLE & TRAVEL	50	250	45	60	60	70	80	40	45	170	50	80	1000
EQUIPMENT & LEASING	500	–	85	–	30	–	–	–	600	–	–	–	1215
TELEPHONE & OFFICE	15	90	10	–	75	20	–	120	15	–	70	30	445
TOTAL OVERHEADS	695	440	355	190	330	355	270	340	1070	450	250	325	5070
MATERIALS	400	80	–	200	–	200	–	170	–	400	–	–	1450
LABOUR/CASH DRAWINGS	160	160	160	160	160	160	160	160	160	160	160	160	1920
TOTAL CASH SPENT	1255	680	515	550	490	715	430	670	1230	1010	410	485	8440
NET PROFIT/NET LOSS	-955	120	385	250	610	135	970	20	-250	290	1190	1315	
CUMULATIVE TOTAL	-955	-835	-450	-200	410	545	1515	1535	1285	1575	2765	4080	

Fig 1 An example of a Cashflow Forecast
You will need to prepare one in order to negotiate overdrafts and loans. A cashflow chart will highlight the seasonal peaks and troughs of your business, when you take into account annual and quarterly bills for services (electricity, insurance, car tax, etc), and seasonal selling periods

The central and most visible part of any presentation should be a clear and fairly concise chart (you don't have to include every single item) forecasting the cashflow and budget control of your business (see Fig 1). Because of the lack of a track record, your cashflow chart will comprise fifteen per cent 'hard' figures (rent, rates etc) and eighty-five per cent 'guesstimate' or educated guesswork (sales, advertising, purchases, etc). Nevertheless, it should provide you with a fairly comprehensive yardstick by which to measure your progress in your first year of trading. Don't worry too much if you find that real life compares unfavourably with your forecast: you won't be able to foresee every eventuality.

Your presentation, both verbal and graphic, should describe the background and the practicalities of your scheme (your qualifications or skills for example), together with an analysis of the market possibilities as you see them. There should also be a fairly clear indication of how much backing and of what sort you would require, and to what use you intend to put it. You will almost certainly be asked what financial resources you already have and what personal commitment you would be willing to offer. Provided the presentation can adequately demonstrate the viability of your scheme, it will have served its purpose.

The amount of start-up capital you will need will probably be relatively modest by normal business standards – I would guess not much more than £12,000 and more likely in the region of £1,500. Why not find out if there is anyone among your family or friends who would be prepared to back you financially? If you do manage to find a private backer, regardless of how close a relative or how good a friend, you must go to a solicitor and get a written agreement drawn up, detailing the period of the loan, the agreed rate of interest and anything else that might at some time in the future be grounds for disagreement between you and your backer.

It might be suggested that your backer becomes a sleeping partner in the business, but you would be wise to bear in mind that sleeping partners have an irritating tendency to wake up just when you don't want them to. Whatever you agree between yourselves, please remember that there is nothing that can create discord between friends and relatives more easily than money, or the lack of it. So the greater the understanding between all parties concerned the better it will be. Try to keep your backers informed at regular intervals of how your business and their money are behaving. If things are going well, they will be delighted; if not, they deserve to be told that their investment is heading for the rocks. Investors as a general rule do not like surprises, especially bad ones. Alternatively you could consider asking your erstwhile backers to help you by guaranteeing a loan from other sources, the implication being that if you cannot meet the repayments, for whatever reason, the lender will be able to call in the debt from your guarantor.

Apart from the general lending opportunities, there are many different types of more specific schemes available to the craftsperson who wishes to set up a new business. There are setting-up grants and various loans offered by several agencies, and though your chances of getting your hands on them are limited, it is always worthwhile applying just in case you happen to strike lucky.

CoSIRA, 141 Castle Street, Salisbury, Wiltshire SP1 3TP (0722 336255) offers various schemes to help small businesses in rural England, and collaborates with several of the major banks in joint lending schemes aimed specifically at small or craft businesses employing twenty or less people. The other regional development agencies also offer financial help and incentives to businesses requiring setting-up loans or workshop grants.

In Scotland, apart from the individual urban and municipal bodies, you will be able to obtain advice from the **Scottish Development Agency**, Roseberry House, Haymarket Terrace, Edinburgh EH12 5EZ (031-337 9595) and the **Highlands and Islands Development Board**, Bridge House, 27 Bank Street, Inverness IV1 1QR (0463 234171). In Wales the **Development Board for Rural Wales**, Ladywell House, Newton, Powys (0686 26965) offers a similar service. In Northern Ireland you should contact the **Local Enterprise Development Unit**, LEDU House, Upper Galwally, Belfast BTB 4TB (0232 691031).

The **Crafts Council**, 8 Waterloo Place, London SW1Y 4AV (01-930 4811) has a limited annual budget that it disburses as workshop grants to craftspeople. However, you will find that it nearly always awards its money to those who have left art colleges within the past two years with professional qualifications.

At present the **Manpower Services Commission** (contact your local Jobcentre) is running its Enterprise Allowance Scheme, which seems to be one of the most successful and generous opportunities on offer to new businesses at the moment. To be eligible you must be between eighteen years old and retirement age; you must have been out of work for a minimum of thirteen weeks, and in receipt of unemployment or supplementary benefit, and you will have to show that you either have £1,000 (perhaps your redundancy pay) or the facility to borrow £1,000 (from your bank?). If you satisfy these requirements and are accepted on to the scheme, you will receive £40 a week in fortnightly payments during your first year as a self-employed person – which could spell the difference between success or failure for many who would not otherwise have the courage or financial resources to start up in business.

There are many other sources of financial assistance to get you going, apart of course from the large private-sector lending companies. For example, if you are in an inner city area you should be able to obtain rent grants from the local authority, whereby they will effectively pay your rent for one or occasionally two years.

Don't despair if you fail to qualify for any of the above goodies. The vast majority of people don't get a penny.

You could, if all else fails, take out a second mortgage on your house (that is, if you have a house) but it is one heck of a gamble to put your house on the line. And is it worth the risk? You are the only person who can make the decision, but I would argue very strongly against it.

Other than by obtaining grants, if I had to come down in favour of just one form of financing a new business venture I would opt for the least adventurous method possible, slow 'organic' growth. In other words, start with as much as you can afford or, if you have an overdraft borrow as little as you need, and slowly build up the business without overstretching your resources. When you purchase goods, utilise the credit period to its maximum, and when you buy equipment, make sure it will recoup its cost quickly. Without being too faddy about it, try to manage your finances carefully and within about two years you should have a healthy little business. One of the reasons why this system appeals to me is that I begrudge paying interest to the banks and other lenders, when my need is so much greater than theirs.

I should add that, whereas this is a relatively good scheme for a very small operation, as soon as your business begins to expand, you will have to borrow from the institutions, but by that time you will be in a much stronger position altogether.

(See chapter 7, 'Who Can Help You?' for possible sources of grants and loans.)

6
Finding Workspace

In its broadest definition, your workspace could be anything from a kitchen-table to a huge factory. And taking into consideration the multitude of different crafts and their diverse, not to mention individual, requirements, either of those two extremes, and everything in between, might be the ideal location for you to practise your skills.

Before you do anything else, you should give some careful thought to the following list of options. It will give you a clearer appreciation of what to look for, when you go out searching for somewhere to set up your business.

● What is the minimum space you will require to work in comfort?
● How soon will it be before you outgrow the premises? (Guess)
● What facilities will you specifically require (single- or triple-phase electricity, gas, etc) and how much will it cost to install?
● Will the neighbours have cause to complain about your noise?
● Will you have cause to complain about anti-social neighbours?
● Do the premises need to be easily accessible?
● Do you wish to sell to the public from the premises?
● Do you want the long-term commitment of a lease? Or a monthly licence (if available) to give you the flexibility of moving on, without the hassle of selling the lease?
● Would you want to buy freehold or perhaps build a workshop on your existing property?
● What can you afford to pay on your own? Could you share premises (and expenses) with other craftspeople?

Once you have realistically defined what would constitute a satisfactory place for you to work in, you will save a great deal of time and trouble by avoiding having to look at premises either totally unsatisfactory or too expensive.

Contrary to popular belief, unless you are specifically looking for a lock-up shop or fairly large industrial premises, you will probably not find workspace through an estate agent. If my own experience is anything to go by, estate agents would rather have a dose of bubonic plague than waste their time on such a small thing as a 500 sq ft workshop.

Fortunately there are several agencies and local government departments who exist almost specifically to help locate premises for craft (or other light industrial) workshops. You can obtain addresses and information by first contacting, among others, the Small Firms Service (Freefone 2444); CoSIRA, 141 Castle Street, Salisbury, Wilts SP1 3TP (0722 336255); the Scottish Development Agency (Small Business Division), Roseberry House, Haymarket Terrace, Edinburgh EH12 5EZ (031-337 9595); the Welsh Development Agency, Treforest Industrial Estate, Pontypridd CF37 5UT (044-385 266); LEDU (for Northern Ireland), LEDU House, Upper Galwally, Belfast BT8 4TB (0232 691031); British Rail Property Board – look in your local telephone directory (ever thought of a railway arch?), and of course your local town hall, which should have someone called an 'Industrial Liaison Officer' or an 'Economic Development Officer', or something along those lines.

All or any of these people should be able to provide you with lists of property available in your area. They should also be in a position to offer you specific advice on any further assistance (advisory and financial) that you might be eligible for. Depending on where you propose setting up your business, you could be able to claim rent-free accommodation for up to two years, or perhaps a period in which the council will waive your rates.

You could also find out from other craftspeople whether they know of any available workspace. Perhaps you might be able to work in someone else's studio or workshop, and share the outgoings between you.

Don't under-estimate the value of the craftworld grapevine. It never ceases to amaze me, the amount of *accurate* information that can be acquired from chatting to other craftspeople. Mind you, there is a fair bit of unsubstantiated rubbish too, so be discriminating.

When you go to visit a prospective workplace, take this checklist with you, so that you will be able to itemise and evaluate what you may need to spend in hidden costs in order to set up shop.

● What facilities are already provided? (Gas, electricity, water, lighting, heating, telephone, toilets etc.)
● How burglar-proof is it already? How much will it cost to make it fully secure? (Very important for jewellers, silversmiths etc)
● Will your customers and suppliers be able to find you?
● Will you have to pay a service charge for common areas?
● Will you, or the premises, be eligible for rate grants, setting-up grants, rate holidays or anything else that may be on offer?

When you add your conclusions from this list to your requirements from the first list, you should be able to obtain a clear indication of whether or not you have found satisfactory and affordable premises.

Don't despair if it takes you a little longer than you had originally allowed to find suitable premises. I would be very surprised if you take the first place that you look at. But allowing for trial, error and a lot of perseverance, you will eventually find a place. Everyone does sooner or later, even if they work in their spare bedroom whilst they are searching.

Should you decide to work from home anyway, you would be well advised to check your lease, or ensure with your landlord that you are not going to contravene umpteen bye-laws and planning rules. Try to behave sensibly and with consideration for family and neighbours, but above all, if all else fails, be discreet.

If you decide to sell your work to the public on a regular basis, you will have to take into account the position of the premises in relation to shopping thoroughfares. There is no point in starving in proud solitude in a low-rent area if no one comes to your shop or even knows of your existence. By that I don't mean that you should go mad and spend a fortune on a 'good' address, even if you have the chance. Weigh up the relative merits of the cost and the position of the premises.

Should the opportunity arise, you may consider buying an established business. If so, it will be either rented on a renewable leasehold or else a freehold property. Apart from the rental or purchase price, you will in all likelihood have to pay for 'fixtures and fittings', 'stock at valuation' and 'goodwill'. The cost of F & F should be fairly easy to negotiate, as indeed will the value of the stock, provided you obtain an independent assessment of its value at 'cost'. Goodwill, on the other hand, is an asset that is always hard to quantify. However, with give-and-take from both sides you will be able to agree a price.

You will require an accountant to study the books and financial records of the business, going back over at least three years. He will try to assess the trends in trading and profitability leading up to your acquisition. Try to find out why the present owners are selling up: their reasons may be a serious disincentive for you to go ahead. Check with the town hall or local authority whether there are any redevelopment plans for the area.

Have a look for yourself at the shops, shopping trends and amenities in the immediate area. See whether there is any serious competition already established nearby. This could be a definite advantage as it will mean that interested customers are already coming to the area and, as a result, may buy from you as well. You should also spend some time discreetly noting how many passers-by go into the shop over a period of time. You won't need to mount round-the-clock surveillance (if you did, someone would be bound to report you to the police for loitering with intent), but you should soon be able to tell whether or not the claims of the sellers are justified.

You might even have thought of combining your workshop with a retail shop or showroom. Provided you don't mind being constantly interrupted by the public, it could be an excellent way of marketing your work. It could also provide you with the opportunity to augment your income by retailing other craftspeople's work as well as your own.

You will find it in your best interest to divide off the shop from the workshop. This will bar, or at least discourage, the over-inquisitive public. Otherwise they will wander blithely into whirring machinery, tip over paint pots or produce their favourite *pièce-de-résistance* of poking their umbrellas through silk screens. The aptitude of the public for finding innocent mischief to get up to is a source of constant wonder. You may even decide to employ someone, full- or part-time, to deal with customers, so as to allow you to get on with your own work.

In your workshop, try to arrange the layout of your equipment with as much thought and common sense as possible. If you need a clean environment for one process, take good care that it will be adequately isolated from other dust-producing processes. Ensure that noxious or inflammable vapours are safely ducted out of the building (and not into the next-door workshop, as in one instance I heard of). Try to maintain a specific and tidy storage area for your raw materials and make sure that all inflammable materials are stored in an approved manner.

From time to time the factory inspectors will spring surprise visits on you, as will the inspectors of the Health and Safety Executive. Whereas they are generally understanding souls who will only make constructive criticism in order to keep you on the straight and narrow, you must keep within the regulations and recommendations of the Factories Act 1961 and the Health & Safety at Work Act 1974, because, if you give them just cause, the inspectors can 'zap' you with no end of contraventions.

Strangely enough, whereas the Health & Safety regulations apply to all workers and premises, the Factories Act applies only to a place of work in which two or more persons work with the permission of, or under agreement with, the owner or occupier. In other words, it does not apply if you work entirely on your own. Nevertheless, as most of the regulations are based on pretty sound judgement, you would be well advised to keep within them.

You will need to allocate an area of your premises for office use. It can be kept to the barest minimum, so long as you will be able to find relevant orders and invoices and all the other scraps of paper that make life so tiresome. A table-top and some manilla folders in cardboard boxes can be as effective for some people as the latest electronic gizmo for others.

Generally speaking, however, I would recommend that you get hold of a typewriter for the occasional business-like business letter. If you can beg, borrow, steal or even purchase (if you have no alternative) a sturdy filing-cabinet, it will prove very useful indeed, together with lots of manilla folders to store and index documents.

Install a telephone in your workshop or office. If you work on your own you will find that an answerphone not only allows you to get out and about, to say nothing of going to the loo undisturbed, but will probably pay for itself with telephoned orders within a very short time. I know that many people hate talking to answerphones (myself included), but I freely admit that I could not survive without one.

You should try to find somewhere or someone with a photocopier, perhaps a nearby office which will only charge you at cost (about 3p per copy) to use their machine. It will prove much cheaper than the photocopier services in the shops or your local library. Once you get the hang of it, a photocopier will prove invaluable for short runs of catalogues, price lists and the like. You might even consider buying or leasing a photocopier of your own, but though the prices are coming down (£500 minimum for a reliable make), they are still a bit pricy.

You will not need a computer, even if you can persuade your spouse or bank manager to the contrary, unless your work specifically requires the application of a computer or a word-processor, or your accounts are already computerised, at this stage in your career. Buy one if you must but, unless you can see it paying for itself fairly quickly, you will find far better uses for your money.

Whilst on the subject of office equipment, you won't need me to remind you about getting ample supplies of printed stationery and all the other consumables that are so essential for the smooth running of a business. Keep a pile of scrap paper on your desk for notes and messages, and tie a pen with a long piece of string to the telephone, so that you will always have it ready to jot down orders over the phone.

Try to make your premises as thief-proof as possible. Unless your insurance company insists otherwise, you will not need to install high-tech ultra-sonic burglar-alarms. In most cases you will find that bars on the windows and a whopping great padlock inserted through a hefty hasp on the door will deter all but the most determined intruder.

Take all the necessary fire precautions, so that a small accident doesn't turn into a major disaster. And make sure that the premises and contents are insured with effect from the date when you sign your tenancy agreement. Don't wait until you move in, as if anything should happen in the interim, you will be held responsible, and that could prove very expensive.

7
Who Can Help You?

Depending on where and how you propose to set up in business, you should find a reasonably wide variety of local, regional, national and, in certain cases, European agencies whose specific function is to offer assistance to people in your position.

As already discussed in the chapter on raising capital, many of these organisations can and do provide financial assistance to new or expanding businesses, but by far and away their major function is to offer expert counselling to new and often inexperienced business management. This counselling embraces all the essential disciplines required to run a business efficiently. You will probably find that you can obtain advice on simple book-keeping and on how to prepare budget forecasts (essential if you apply for a bank loan, for example). They should also be in a position to give you fairly accurate and up-to-date information about exports or marketing in general. In some cases you may be able to take advantage of free exhibition space at expensive trade shows or other major events.

I seriously recommend you give these experts a call – at this stage in your career you will need as many 'friends' as you can get. But when you go to seek their advice, keep one thought uppermost in your mind: With the best will in the world, they can only give disinterested advice. If you follow their advice blindly and come unstuck, you will find it extremely difficult to lay the blame at the expert's door. I would not say that it cannot be done, but it is a pretty hollow sort of victory if you do succeed. Therefore, go along and seek advice; listen and, if need be, act on that advice. But take it with just the tiniest pinch of salt, because one of the pleasures and perils of being self-employed is that you, and only you, are ultimately responsible for the decisions that you take. There are many alternative sources of help that you can turn to, apart from the 'official' agencies, boards and schemes. You are probably making use of some of them already. For example:

LIBRARIES AND MUSEUMS

Your local public library is a source for all kinds of information. Why spend money on reference books for a particular project if you can borrow them free from the library? Similarly with museums. If you are fortunate enough to have a museum of either general or specific interest nearby, you will probably be allowed to use its reference library for your research. If it is too far away or if it is inconvenient for you to visit, you could always phone or write to the curator concerned, detailing your enquiry. In most cases they will do their utmost to help you.

COLLEGES

Technical colleges, polytechnics and art colleges can also be approached. It helps if you are an ex-student or if you know someone connected with the college. When dealing with colleges or similar institutions, it is always a case of whom you know, not what you know, that gets results. Provided you approach them properly, they might well be able to offer you valuable technical advice, and in exceptional circumstances you might be allowed to use their facilities.

You might consider joining an evening class at a local art college, partly to improve your skills but also to give you an opportunity to cultivate useful contacts against the day when you might need to call on them. Obviously there are no hard-and-fast rules, but if the powers-that-be think you have a talent worth helping, they will often be more than generous with their time and advice. Needless to say, you should never give them the impression that you are taking advantage of their good services (as if you would!). There may also be the opportunity for you to offer work-experience to college students. Apart from helping to maintain good contacts, your business could benefit from the fresh expertise in technical or commercial subjects that the students would bring with them. However, the drawback is that they might be utterly useless.

LOCAL GROUPS

If there is a local arts association in your vicinity, you could consider joining it, though from what little contact I have had with local organisations of that kind, they tend to be cliquey. With a few exceptions, they are rarely more than well-meaning 'talking shops', strong on committees and weak on practicalities, and I doubt that you will have time for theorising once you have started up in business.

Local craft guilds are more positive in their approach and will also give you the chance to meet other craftspeople in your locality. Whereas they will be strong in organising local summer or Christmas events, they are as a rule rather parochial.

NATIONAL GROUPS

You could of course apply to join a national crafts guild or association related to your specific interest. Generally speaking, they offer members a nationwide network of craftspeople to whom an individual can turn for advice. Making crafts can be an extremely solitary occupation, and it is quite comforting to know that there are other people out there who have to cope with problems and pressures not dissimilar to your own. A worthwhile guild should keep the membership informed about what is happening in their craft-related world. They may also provide an opportunity for craftspeople to exchange ideas and sell equipment and materials to one another.

Should you decide to become part of a crafts association or guild, try to find one that places its emphasis on excellence and a high standard of craftsmanship, because, above all else, that is what we are all concerned with (see list of craft associations, page 129).

THE CRAFTS COUNCIL

I sometimes feel that the best thing about the Crafts Council is simply that it exists. It doesn't seem to do much in practical terms to help the majority of individual craftspeople, particularly if you haven't been to art school. And nobody could accuse it of reckless spending when it disburses the few grants at its disposal. Yet one can forgive it nearly everything because its heart is definitely in the right place. Until a couple of years ago, it was widely felt in the crafts community (justifiably or not) that unless you were an esoteric ceramicist or lute-maker the Crafts Council would not be interested in you. Recently, however, it seems to have undergone a mild conversion, the old elitist attitudes have gone, hopefully for ever, and the Crafts Council is much more involved with mainstream contemporary crafts. At its headquarters at 12 Waterloo Place, London SW1 4AU, the Council maintains a comprehensive slide library of British crafts produced by selected makers. There is also a crafts register open to all craftspeople, in which you should make it a priority to be included. The Crafts Council also has a programme of craft exhibitions, both, in its own gallery and in collaboration with regional arts associations around the country.

LOCAL GOVERNMENT AUTHORITY

Your local authority should be able to offer you a great deal of help when you are getting started. Many authorities will offer financial aid in the form of rent grants or rate 'holidays'. They will also, to a greater or lesser extent, be able to offer you a business advisory service to help you to get to grips with the technicalities of business procedure. Every local authority has different priorities depending on the local conditions, and the help offered varies considerably, but you should contact your local town hall as soon as possible following your decision to start up your business, in order to find out what, if anything, is available.

For the rest, I have drawn up a list of the major national and regional organisations which may be in a position to assist you, together with a brief resumé of what is on offer from each. Owing to the constantly changing state of public sector spending, you should ring up each individual organisation and request that they send you up-to-date information with regard to what they have on offer.

Sources of Help

The British Council, 65 Davies Street, London W1Y 2AA (01-499 8011) Promotes cultural, educational and technical co-operation between Britain and other countries. It arranges exhibitions of British arts in foreign countries and in certain circumstances offers travel grants to craftspeople.

British Overseas Trade Board, 1 Victoria Street, London SW1Y 0ET (01-215 7877) Part of the Department of Trade. General advice to exporters. Sponsors trade missions and offers subsidies to exporters who go to foreign trade exhibitions; gives introductions to potential foreign buyers.

British Standards Institution, 2 Park Street, London W1A 2BS (01-629 9000) and Test House, Maylands Avenue, Hemel Hempstead, Herts HP2 4SQ (0442 3111) It is required by law for many products to keep within British and foreign safety standards. You will find that many of the standards are infuriatingly non-specific, and the people at the BSI head office don't help much, but the Test House will analyse and test products that are sent to them by manufacturers (for a fee).

Co-Operative Development Agency, Broadmead House, 21 Panton Street, London SW1Y 4DR (01-839 2988) An advisory body set up by the government to promote the co-operative sector in the UK. It offers introductions to local CDAS, information about co-ops, advice on how to set up a co-operative business, training, registration to incorporate a co-op business, etc.

CoSIRA, 141 Castle Street, Salisbury, Wiltshire SP1 3TP (0722 336255) The Council for Small Industries in Rural Areas is an agency of the Development Commission. Its objective is to revitalise country areas in England by helping small firms to succeed. It provides technical and professional advice, business management advice, financial aid in the form of loans and grants, skill training courses and a range of craft-related publications.

The Crafts Council, 12 Waterloo Place, London SW1Y 4AU (01-930 4811) Offers financial aid to craftspeople in the form of setting-up schemes and workshop grants. Maintains a register of crafts and an extensive slide library. Publishes various craft-related books and publications. The Crafts Council operates only in England and Wales.

The Design Council, Design Centre, 28 Haymarket, London SW1Y 4SU (01-839 8000) The Design Council selects products to be included on its design register. Selected products may display the famous Design Centre label and are sometimes sold and exhibited at the Design Centre. The idiosyncratic behaviour, and often élitist attitude with which the Design Council tends to arbitrate on 'good taste' annoys many craftspeople and delights others.

Development Board for Rural Wales, Ladywell House, Newton, Powys (0686 26965) Advice and financial aid for small businesses in rural Wales.

Export Credit Guarantee Department, PO Box 272, Aldermanbury House, Aldermanbury Square, London EC2P 2EL (01-606 6699) A government department that offers payment guarantees to exporters.

Highland Craftpoint, Beauly, Inverness-shire IV4 7EH (0463 782578) Funded in part by the Highlands & Islands Development Board and the Scottish Development Agency, its primary function is to assist the development of craft-related businesses. It offers a fully integrated package of professional services encompassing training, development, marketing and general business information to craftspeople throughout Scotland, though in practical terms it tends to restrict its services to the area covered by the HIDB: Shetland, Orkney, Western Isles, Highland Region, Argyll, Bute, Arran and the Cumbraes.

Financial aid is not directly available but on behalf of the HIDB it undertakes the technical assessment of applications for loans and grants made by new and established businesses in its region and will help applicants prepare their cases.

Highlands & Islands Development Board, Bridge House, 27 Bank Street, Inverness IV1 1QR (0463 234171) Advice and financial aid for small businesses in the Scottish highlands and islands. With regard to crafts the board works in conjunction with Highland Craftpoint.

Local Enterprise Development Unit (LEDU), LEDU House, Upper Galwally, Belfast BT8 4TB (0232 691031) The government-sponsored Small Business Agency for Northern Ireland. It offers advice and financial aid to small businesses.

LEntA, 69 Cannon Street, London EC4N 5AB (01-236 2675) The London Enterprise Agency is funded by the private sector to help encourage the creation and growth of small businesses in London. Offers business training courses, 'Design Enterprise Programme', counselling, 'marriage bureau' to introduce small firms to potential investors, small units to let in Inner London.

Manpower Services Commission (MSC) – contact via your local Jobcentre. A government agency that offers the Enterprise Allowance Scheme to help the unemployed start up their own businesses.

Mid-Wales Development, Ladywell House, Newtown, Powys SY16 1JB (0686 26965) Offers a full range of advice and financial aid to small businesses in Mid-Wales. (See Development Board for Rural Wales.)

Patent Office & Industrial Property & Copyright Dept, 25 Southampton Buildings, Chancery Lane, London WC2A 1AY (01-405 8721) Information about patenting your product.

Scottish Development Agency (Small Business Division), Roseberry House, Haymarket Terrace, Edinburgh EH12 5EZ (031-337 9595) A wide range of advice and aid for small businesses in Scotland. It also runs the Scottish Trade Development Centre in London as a showplace for products produced in Scotland.

Small Firms Service, twelve centres around Britain – call Freefone 2444 to contact your nearest branch. Part of the Department of Trade and Industry that offers a wide range of information and business counselling to small businesses. The Service operates through a nationwide network of twelve Small Firms Centres and eighty Area Counselling Offices.

URBED, 99 Southwark Street, London SE1 0JF (01-928 9515) A non-profit-making company supported by the MSC which specialises in programmes that combine the resources of the private and public sectors to create employment and regenerate run-down areas. Offers business training programmes for new business people.

Welsh Development Agency, Treforest Industrial Estate, Pontypridd CF37 5UT (044-385 266) Advice and aid to businesses in Wales in conjunction with the other Welsh agencies.

The majority of the above organisations do not have either the time or the patience to discuss abstract business propositions, so in order to save time and effort (yours as much as theirs), try to prepare a carefully considered presentation of your scheme to demonstrate that you have done your basic groundwork. If, however, the 'experts' pour cold water on your plans, which they often do, don't let this discourage you from trying to fulfil your dreams: it is your life, not theirs.

And, of course, always bear in mind that other craftspeople will be able to offer you a great deal of advice, encouragement and help.

II
GOING INTO PRODUCTION

8
Boss, Worker, Teaboy

I doubt that you will need reminding that, when you decide to become a self-employed craftsperson, every tiny act or decision rests on one person – you.

For those who have experienced the world of industry this can come as a bit of a shock. The discovery that you are no longer an insignificant cog in a large machine is quite daunting. However, the important thing is for you quickly to come to terms with the situation as it exists, and capitalise on it. Firstly, rather than ignore your limitations, try to understand them. It will make your life much easier if you can work within set parameters of ability, and as you learn from experience and grow increasingly confident, you will soon find ways of broadening your capabilities.

Try to appreciate what is expected of you by your customers, both as a skilled craftsperson and as a businessperson who is to be relied upon. At the same time, without being too philosophical, try to understand what you expect of yourself. Above all, be honest, if only with yourself. Nobody expects you to be the embodiment of all the earthly skills from day one of your new career. Far too many highly talented craftspeople have given up without a struggle because they haven't managed to live up to their own expectations. Give yourself a fair chance to achieve the success that you deserve, regardless of whether your criteria of success are those of fame or fortune.

If you are going to work entirely on your own, you will have to learn very quickly how to structure your time, or your working day will slip by without anything whatsoever being achieved. Make it a rule to try to earn something every single day – not necessarily by actually selling, but simply by producing something that is saleable. At first you may find it necessary to plan your day (or week) on a piece of paper, detailing orders to fill, people to contact and all the other chores that occupy one's time, including paperwork and correspondence. Allocate periods in the day for each of these activities, and try to keep to your schedule.

From time to time you will probably have to stop being a craftsperson and instantly become an accounts clerk or sales director. At first you will find this sort of gear-changing an intrusion, but you will soon find that occasionally changing the pace and nature of your work will not only stop you going stale but afford you a new perspective on your work. It is easy to get stuck in a rut when you are on your own, and, even if it is a comfortable rut, in the long term it will have an unproductive effect on your work.

If you are going to market your own work, you will soon pick up the rudiments of psychological warfare that are the stock-in-trade of the ace salesperson. Don't make the mistake, however, of letting the customer forget that you are the person responsible for creating the product, because, in the world of arts and crafts, if you are too slick in your sales presentation it will tend to put people off. The customer sometimes needs to be reminded that you have sawdust on your boots (in a manner of speaking).

As a self-employed craftsperson you will have no alternative but to be a jack-of-all-trades. You will almost inevitably be initiated into the ancient art of 'bodging', which in its present context means the ability to improvise. So long as you are reconciled to the first law of commerce – 'whatever can go wrong, will go wrong' – you should be able to cope with every eventuality. By that I mean that you must be adept at the string and Sellotape technology of make-do and mend, because even if you could afford to get everything repaired properly, you can be certain that equipment breaks down with exquisite timing (usually at 5.35 pm on a Friday) just as you are trying to meet a deadline.

When you are self-employed, you must learn to stand up for your rights. If that is not in your nature, you should find a friend who will argue on your behalf. You would be amazed what miracles a judicious outburst of outraged indignation will produce when you are dealing with suppliers of faulty goods or customers who are slow to pay. Obviously you must use your discretion, but always remember that nobody is going to bother about you if you don't care about yourself. So be charming and tactful, but above all be insistent.

While on the subject of protecting your interests, you ought to be aware that the world is full of plagiarists who know no shame at all in ripping off other people's designs, and usually badly at that. Should you have had the foresight and money to copyright your work, so much the better, but most craftspeople don't bother. If anything like that does happen to you, in such a way that it could seriously affect your livelihood, spare no effort to put a stop to it as soon as possible, even to the extent of taking legal advice. All but the most determined or brazen pirates will be deterred by a stern letter from your solicitor, even though you may have no intention of taking the matter to court.

The worst thing about being your own boss is that you won't have anyone to blame for foul-ups, other than yourself. And if you employ others to work for you, you will have to reconcile yourself to the fact that at the end of the week your employees will probably be earning more than you – added to which, you have the responsibility of running the business.

All of the above, and more, lies in store for you from the moment you start up on your own. Don't let it put you off. It is a bit like being a juggler: to keep everything up in the air and spinning, you will have to be extremely flexible in your approach to everything connected with your business. On no account allow yourself to get into a panic, and if things look as though they are getting out of control, find someone to discuss it with before it is too late. Believe it or not, things are rarely as bad as they first appear. So long as you enjoy the challenge, even bad days can often be turned to your advantage.

9
Employing Staff

As your business grows, you may have to consider employing people to help you. Don't be under the misapprehension that being an employer is going to be easy. It is not. Nevertheless, if you really want your business to expand, it will be almost inevitable that you will employ others in one capacity or another.

Why and when you decide to take on staff, or to farm jobs out to homeworkers and sub-contractors, will depend largely on the speed with which your business develops, and whether or not you can cope satisfactorily on your own. You may decide that you are too tied up doing tedious, repetitive chores, when your time could be spent more profitably concentrating on the processes that particularly demand your skills. If you run a shop or gallery you may need a sales assistant, even if it is only to free you to get out and see suppliers. Whatever the reason, the solution to your problem is to employ staff.

Ask nearly any employer whether it is easy to get hold of reliable, hard-working staff and the answer in most cases will be a depressing 'no'. Only part of the problem, however, lies with the employee. A good working team demands considerable input from the employer too. Too many bosses fail to realise that although to themselves their businesses are the most important things in the world, as far as their staff are concerned it is just a job, and no more.

Try to motivate your workers. Give them responsibility if you feel they justify it. Although there will be hiccoughs along the way, if you can manage to work as one cohesive team it will make for an easier and more profitable life for all concerned.

When you find staff, you owe it to yourself to check their references – if need be by telephoning their former employer. Be rather wary of anyone coming along with too glowing a reference, especially one that is carefully non-specific as to the reasons for leaving; if they were that good, why did their former employer let them go?

The next question is whether you can provide enough work to keep your employees fully occupied all week, every week. This is absolutely vital because from the moment you employ staff, the most expensive component in your pricing structure will be labour.

The two most basic mistakes you can make with employees are to allow them to sit around with nothing to do or to get them to produce stock speculatively to stop them from getting bored. By so doing you will be using up your resources at no profit to your business whatsoever.

If you have enough work for a full-time employee, so much the better; if not, you might consider the alternatives of part-timers, outworkers and, though strictly speaking not employees, sub-contractors.

The only proviso I would make is that you must be vigilant about quality control. In an ideal world one should not accept any shoddy work at all; however, reality dictates that you may have to accept a small percentage (two to four per cent) of rejects, particularly from your outworkers. You will of course allow for this in the costing of your product when you come to fix the selling price. By the same token it is up to you to ensure that your workers (employed or contracted) are not cheating you by using your materials and/or designs to make goods either for themselves or for resale. This is common practice in the fashion industry, and nothing so far has led me to believe that it doesn't happen elsewhere.

HIRING

In law, as soon as you offer somebody a job, whether the offer is written or verbal, there exists between you a contract of employment. You will then be required by law to provide the employee with written details setting out the main terms and conditions of the contract within thirteen weeks of their starting work.

This applies to all employees (full-time, part-time, outworkers), the notable exceptions being: employees who work for sixteen hours a week or less; your spouse; a person employed for a specific contract not expected to be more than twelve weeks duration (unless employed for longer than twelve weeks), and independent contractors. If you do not supply a contract of employment, you will be laying yourself open to future problems should an employee decide to go to an industrial tribunal with a complaint. Industrial relations (for such it is) are always highlighted when there is discontent at work. Far better to set out in writing, clearly and unambiguously, the terms and conditions of employment before your working relationship has a chance to sour.

Every contract must include the following details:

- Name of employer
- Name of employee
- Job title/description of function
- Rate of pay/pay period (hourly, weekly, monthly)
- Normal working hours or rules regarding hours of work
- Holiday, and rate of holiday pay if any
- Rules for absence through sickness or injury, and rates of pay
- Pension details
- The length of notice the employee is entitled to receive and must give
- Disciplinary rules that affect the employee
- Provision for a complaints and/or grievance procedure for the employee

If you make any alteration to the terms of the contract, you are required to notify the employee in writing within one month of the change.

When you engage staff, whether on a full-time or part-time basis (and you are their sole employer), you must ask them for their P45 parts 2 and 3, which their previous employer should have given them. This form will provide you with details of the employee's tax code and pay to date. Immediately upon your receiving the P45, you are required to follow the instructions on part 2 and send part 3 to the tax office whilst also preparing a tax-deduction card in accordance with the instructions that you will be given by the tax office.

In the event of your employee not producing a P45 (if working for more than one week and earning more than £38.50), the employee must complete a P15 (coding claim) and a P46 (1982), both of which are to be sent to the tax office as soon as possible.

I would urge you, however, to seek expert advice from your tax office and accountant with regard to the detailed information that you will need in dealing with PAYE, National Insurance and all other matters relating to your obligations as an employer.

FIRING

If you thought that hiring employees would be difficult, dismissing them is often far worse. Unfortunately we are never at our best when this particular situation arises, yet sometimes it is necessary to get rid of staff, and it won't do any good to put it off simply because you cannot bear the thought of upsetting anyone.

As an employer you are required to give the following minimum periods of notice to employees who have been continuously employed for four weeks or more:

Period of employment	Minimum notice
4 weeks – less than 2 years	1 week
2 years – less than 12 years	1 week + 1 week for each year of employment
12 years or more	12 weeks

An employee who has been continuously employed for four

weeks or more is required to give one week's notice. For gross misconduct on the part of the employee, the notice rights do not apply. Grounds for dismissal for gross misconduct tend to be somewhat ambiguous, however, and after the heat of the moment has abated you may be called upon to justify your actions should the sacked employee claim unfair dismissal.

Employees have the right not to be unfairly dismissed only if they have been employed for two years (in firms with twenty employees or less), except in cases of unlawful sexual or racial discrimination or trade union activity.

Both employer and employee may accept payment in lieu of notice, and should you wish to extend the periods of notice, there is nothing to stop you.

In all matters relating to employment, you must seek expert advice, or you could easily find yourself embroiled in a no-win situation because of what may have started as a simple misunderstanding with one of your employees.

You may obtain information leaflets and advice from the Department of Employment (go to your nearest Jobcentre) and also from ACAS, 11 St James's Square, London SW1Y 4LA.

10
Suppliers

You will very soon discover, if you have not already done so, that from the moment you decide to be a self-employed, self-sufficient craftsperson you are totally dependent on all kinds of people. So much for self-sufficiency.

Chief among the people on whom your business depends are your suppliers. Whether they are wholesalers of bulk raw materials or other craftspeople from whom you purchase part-made or wholly made goods, a large part of your ultimate success will be based on a good working relationship between you and your suppliers.

Your pricing structure will be dictated to a considerable extent by the cost of raw materials and consumables that you have to purchase. Therefore it will be in your best interest to make every effort to find the most advantageous prices available. It is nearly always a false economy to sacrifice quality for cost. By all means buy in goods and materials at the lowest possible price, but try to ensure that the quality of what you are buying is up to standard. There is little point in spending long hours and hard work in producing a craft item if the basic materials are shoddy or not suited to their purpose. You will find that for only a slightly greater initial capital outlay you should be able to create something worthy of your efforts.

If you take the trouble to shop around, you will be amazed at the wide range of different prices for essentially similar goods or services. Now that you are engaged in 'trade', you will not be restricted to buying solely from retailers. Indeed, you will now be able to buy from the sources that supply the retailers from whom you have bought in the past.

Suppliers

The amount of discount for which you might qualify will depend largely on the size of your order: the larger the order, the greater the discount that you will be entitled to receive. The cheapest prices are usually quoted as 'wholesale', 'trade' or 'bulk'. Do not be afraid of approaching wholesalers: they are, after all, only salespeople like yourself. Most wholesale establishments will insist on your placing a minimum order, though, as this is usually carriage paid, it can be of benefit to craftspeople in rural areas or for those without suitable transport of their own.

If you find that the minimum order requirement is more than you either need or can afford, you might consider sharing an order with a fellow craftsperson. Alternatively a group of you might get together to bulk-buy certain materials, so each of you benefits by the lower unit price. Be advised, however, not to over-purchase when buying in stock simply because the price is rock bottom. There is a danger of tying up valuable capital in surplus stock that you may not require for years to come. I speak somewhat ruefully from personal experience. When I started up my own business, I ordered a quantity of masking tape from a sales rep who called at my workshop. The price was very competitive, so I suppose I was over-enthusiastic when I placed my order. Every year since then, whenever I carry out my end of year stock-take, the pile of masking tape never seems to diminish. I could argue that I have hedged against inflation by stocking up on tape, but the truth of the matter is that I made the classic mistake of tying up capital unnecessarily. We all make this mistake, but unless you are totally profligate, it should not prove too disastrous to your business. Try to be aware of the false economy of over-purchasing, especially if the goods in question have a limited shelf-life.

Always be on the look-out for alternative sources of supply, because if you have a sole supplier for some essential material and it ceases trading, you could find yourself in a potentially disastrous situation. You might even be forced to stop manufacturing or trading because of your inability to maintain the supply of materials necessary for your work.

One of the best ways of discovering where to find reliable suppliers is by asking other craftspeople, most of whom will be only too happy to reveal their sources to you, provided you approach them in the right way. If you give people the impression that you are a threat to their business, or that you may want to copy their work (not of course that you would), you certainly won't get any help from them, and quite rightly so. Therefore in this, as in all else, use your common sense.

As a business you should be able to arrange credit from those suppliers with whom you deal on a regular basis. The usual practice is for the firm in question to ask you for a couple of trade references, or perhaps a trade reference and a bank reference, in order to satisfy itself as to your credit-worthiness. You will find that normal trade terms allow you thirty days credit, after which you will be expected to pay the outstanding debt, much as you would expect your own customers to pay you. In many cases you may also be offered the opportunity of a percentage discount (usually two to five per cent for payment in seven days) for early settlement of bills. It is then up to you to decide which is of greater benefit to you.

You should use credit whenever and wherever possible. If you can manage it sensibly, it will help your cashflow by minimising the time during which you will be committing your capital before you get paid by the people whom you supply.

In your early days it will be in your best interest to establish a track record as a good risk with your suppliers, by ensuring that you pay up on time. By so doing you will be able to increase your credit limit as and when you will need to in the future, and if you have good mutual relations with your suppliers, they will be prepared to help you in all kinds of ways, such as helping you to prototype new designs or perhaps involving you in joint advertising promotions.

In order to avoid misunderstandings when goods or services are supplied to you, you should check every docket, invoice and bill against deliveries as soon as they arrive. At the same time you would be well advised to check the quality of the goods. In the event of there being something wrong, your case for complaint, even if justified, will be drastically reduced if you leave it for more than a week after receipt of delivery. This is not to say that your statutory rights are in any way affected by not complaining immediately, and whilst it is strictly speaking neither legal nor ethical, you may decide as an extreme sanction to withhold or delay payment on faulty goods. But it makes more sense to try to sort out any problems quickly and amicably, since you will presumably wish to continue dealing with the supplier in question.

There will be occasions when you may inadvertently forget to pay a supplier on time. Far be it from me to suggest that you try any of the reasons (excuses?) for late payment listed in chapter 21: as a creative craftsperson, you should be able to make up a few good ones of your own.

Sources of Supply

This is by no means a complete list of craft material suppliers but it may help you to get started.

Artists' Materials
L. Cornelissen & Son, 22 Great Queen Street, London WC2

Carving & Sculpting Equipment
Alec Tiranti, 70 High Street, Theale, Reading, Berks RG7 5AR

Craft Materials & Accessories
A. J. Handicraft Supplies Ltd, Vauxhall Industrial Estate, Canterbury, Kent CT1 1YY (0227 69888)
Dryad, PO Box 38, Northgates, Leicester LE1 9BU (0533 50405)
W. Hobby Ltd, Knights Hill Square, London SE27 0HH (01-761 4247)

Enamelling
The Enamel Shop, Craft O'Hans (London), 21 Macklin Street, London WC2B 5NH (01-242 7043)

Glass (Specialist)
Rankin Glass, 24–34 Pearson Street, London E2

Jewellers' Equipment
Blundells & Son Ltd, 199 Wardour Street, London W1
London Bullion Ltd, 193 Wardour Street, London W1

Leather & Leatherworkers' Equipment
J. T. Batchelor, 10 Culford Mews, London N1 4DZ (01-254 2962)

Paints & Varnishes
J. W. Bollom & Co Ltd, PO Box 78, Beckenham, Kent BR3 4BL
(01-658 2299)
Humbrol, Marfleet, Hull, N. Humberside HU9 5NE (0482
701191)
John Myland, 80 Norwood High Street, London SE27 9NW
(01-670 9161)

Potters' Materials & Equipment
The Fulham Pottery, 184 New King's Road, London SW6 (01-731
2167)
Potclays, Brickkiln Lane, Etruria, Stoke-on-Trent, Staffs

Screenprinting Equipment
Sericol, 24 Parsons Green Lane, London SW6 (01-731 3388)

Self-Adhesive Address Labels
Able-Label, Steepleprint Ltd, Earls Barton, Northampton NN6
0LS

Soft Craft & Toy Materials
Atlascraft Ltd, 17 Ludlow Hill Road, Melton Road, West
Bridgford, Nottingham
B. Brown (Holborn) Ltd, 32 Greville Street, London EC1 (01-242
4311)
Beckfoot Mill, Howden Road, Silsden, near Keighley, W.
Yorkshire BD20 0HA (0535 53358)

Timber

Mouldings: F. W. Mason & Sons Ltd, Colwick, Nottingham NG4 2EQ (0602 611555)

Hardwoods: Moss & Co, Dimes Place, 104–6 King Street, London W6

Veneers: The Art Veneers Co Ltd, Industrial Estate, Mildenhall, Suffolk

11
Taxation

This chapter should be read as a guide to the various forms of taxation that apply to a small business. Due to the complex nature of taxation in general, and business taxation in particular, you ought to seek expert advice as to how you and your particular business are affected.

Chapter 2 tells how to set about choosing a firm of accountants who will look after your interests. It will be up to it not only to advise you on all matters connected with taxation (National Insurance, PAYE, VAT, etc) but also to intercede on your behalf with the tax authorities in order to obtain the best deal for you in relation to your tax liabilities.

Accountants are not cheap, but you should find that in the long term they will almost certainly be cost-effective in relation to what they will save you in tax. If you do engage a firm of accountants to look after your interests, the tax authorities will usually correspond with it directly, rather than through you, although you will still be sent the annual tax return forms to fill in and sign. Don't forget, however, that the tax authorities will still hold you responsible for all your tax returns and claims, and not your accountants.

INCOME TAX

If you are proposing to start up as a sole trader or in a partnership, you are required by law to advise your local inspector of taxes as soon as you commence business. To do this you should complete the Inland Revenue form 41G, obtainable from the Small Firms Service (see chapter 7) or from your local inspector of taxes. The form is also included in a booklet published by the Inland Revenue, *Starting In Business* (IR28), available free of charge from your local tax office.

A sole trader is subject to income tax under Schedule D on the profits from the business (after deductions have been made for personal allowances and normal business expenditure). As a sole trader you will not receive a wage deducted from the business's profits; instead, 'drawings' are made from the business which, from the point of view of the taxman, are considered advances on future profits. Income tax is not deducted from the drawings but calculated on the business profits before the drawings are made.

The same applies to a partnership, although in a partnership a single assessment of income tax is made and, as with all the other liabilities of a partnership, should one or more of the partners fail to pay his or her share, the full balance of the income tax assessment has to be met by the others.

A limited company is treated by the Inland Revenue in an entirely different way from sole traders and partnerships. Apart from the fact that the accounts have to be audited by a qualified accountant, limited companies are also liable for corporation tax, calculated on the profits of the company at set percentage rates depending on the size of the profits.

Whilst there is nothing to stop your dealing direct with the Inland Revenue, it would be in your best interest, from the point of view of time and money, to hand the negotiations over to accountants. Provided you have faith in your accountants, let them get on with it.

Some people have the totally false assumption that new businesses are not liable for tax in their first few years. Let me categorically refute that idea. Many, if not most, new businesses *pay* no tax in their first few years – an entirely different matter. This is because the Inland Revenue will have managed to assess the first year's tax liabilities only after the end of the first financial year; also, because you pay tax only on profits, and as most businesses make an overall loss in their first year there will be no tax to pay. You will then be in a position to carry forward previous years' losses to offset future profits, as a result of which you may end up not having to pay income tax for your first couple of years. If, on the other hand, you have made a net profit in your first year, you will, without any doubt, be liable for tax. It is for this reason that most accountants will suggest that your business shows a loss for the first year of trading.

Should you find that, due to ignorance or oversight, you have failed to complete your tax returns but that the Inland Revenue send you an assessment anyway, go directly to an accountant to sort your books out. If you decide to pay the first estimated assessment, because it is temptingly low, you will be laying up a store of trouble for yourself in the future. Let me explain: the first year, the Revenue may assess your tax liability at, say, £400, which you consider a real bargain compared with your sales turnover. You may agree to that first assessment and pay up. If you don't bother to make a return for the second year, they may send you an assessment for £800 (for example), which may or may not be a fair guess at your true tax liability. But if you let things slide for a third or fourth year they will eventually hit you with an assessment for several thousand pounds, which will 'knock your socks off'! You will then be in the impossible position of having to prepare three or four years' accounts within the thirty days that you have to appeal or else having to pay a tax assessment that could wipe you out. If this has left you fuddled, don't worry. It is expressly to contend with matters like this that you should engage an accountant; after all, they're trained for it.

If you decide to work from home, you should be able to claim back a proportion of your overheads (rates, lighting, heating, cleaning, etc) against tax, calculated on either the floor area or the number of rooms used for business purposes. You can also claim a proportion of the costs of rent and telephone (usually up to a maximum of two-thirds of the total). However, as this might make you liable for capital gains tax should you decide to sell your property, you must consult your accountant before making a decision.

PAYE

If you employ staff, you will be responsible for deducting income tax and national insurance contributions from their wages at source and paying it monthly to the Inland Revenue. This method of tax deduction is called Pay As You Earn and is applicable to all employees, whether they are full-time, part-time or (as in many cases) outworkers. If you have formed a limited company and receive a salary from it, you too will be liable for PAYE deductions.

When you decide to employ staff, you would be well advised to contact your local inspector of taxes to obtain up-to-date information and advice regarding PAYE. Similarly your local DHSS will provide you with information on National Insurance.

VAT

VAT is a sales tax levied on goods and services (with certain exceptions) at each stage of the production and distribution chain, and it can be claimed back by purchasers who are registered for VAT.

You will be liable for VAT registration when your turnover exceeds a pre-determined limit for the end of any three month or twelve month period (the limit for 1985–6 was £6,200 for a quarter, £18,700 for four quarters). If you have *any* grounds for believing that you will exceed these limits, you will be liable for registration.

You may register voluntarily for VAT, even if your turnover does not require you to do so. This is done by completing form VAT 1 and sending it to HM Customs & Excise, which administers VAT. The head office for VAT administration is at King's Beam House, 39–41 Mark Lane, London EC3R 7HE (01-626 1515); the address and telephone number of your local VAT sub-office will be found in your local telephone directory. In this instance the registration will normally continue for two years, after which you can apply to deregister. Before making any decision you should talk it over with your accountant or business adviser.

For a registered business, VAT works as follows. When you purchase goods or services, an element of the price you pay will consist of VAT (fifteen per cent at time of writing); this is called 'input tax', which you can claim back from Customs & Excise. When you sell goods to the consumer, an element of the price you charge will also consist of VAT; this is 'output tax', which you pay to Customs & Excise. At the end of each calendar quarter you deduct one from the other and, depending on which is the greater, you either pay the difference to the VATman or claim it back.

If you propose to sell your crafts abroad (inside or outside the EEC), you will probably find that it is in your interest to be VAT-registered, because, whilst you can claim back the VAT on your purchases, you will not be charging VAT on your export sales, the result being that you will be a net claimant for VAT repayments. You will also find it to your advantage to register if you sell to retailers, because, if they are also registered, they will be able to claim back the VAT on what they buy from you. You meanwhile can claim on your purchases. The only person who ends up being lumbered with paying VAT and not getting it back is the poor old consumer at the end of the distribution chain.

The major drawback in being VAT-registered is that you will be involved in more paperwork because of the requirement to keep proper records. You will also have periodic visits from VAT officers to check that your VAT records are in order.

12
Why Does Everyone Get a Wage Except Me?

During your first few years of being self-employed it will seem that everyone gets paid and earns a living except you. Your suppliers get paid (I hope), your printer gets paid, your landlord gets paid and even your employees get paid. Money comes in and goes out easily, but little of it stays in your bank account. In this instance appearances are not deceptive. Until you have developed a market for your product and can create a regular rhythm of work that co-ordinates purchases to productivity and sales, you will be working on a shoestring.

Don't let this put you off the idea of going ahead with your plans. If anything, you will find that the simple need to make and sell enough to keep going for another month, and another after that, will drive you to do some of your most creative work – sheer desperation, rather than necessity, being the mother of invention.

The early period that you spend as a craftsperson may be the first opportunity you have of literally getting your hands 'dirty'. Make the most of it, because it is quite possible that in a relatively short time your business will have prospered to the extent that you will be employing staff to do the practical work, whilst you concentrate on design or marketing. Hard as it may be for you to imagine now, you will look back with fond longing to your early days, when everything was apparently so simple. You will of course have suppressed the memories of how depressing it was to be down to your last couple of quid.

As soon as you start up in business on your own, you will

73

notice that you do not fall ill as often as before. This is not due to the fact that craftspeople are any healthier than the rest of humanity; the opposite is probably true. The simple fact is that you will be too busy working to worry about a sore throat or terminal beri-beri; apart from that, if you do stay in bed feeling sorry for yourself, no one is going to earn your living for you; thus leaving you with the complication of starvation on top of what laid you low in the first place.

If you are really finding it impossible to make ends meet, you should seriously consider subsidising your craft by doing other work on a part-time basis. This will fall into three basic categories. Firstly you could try to do work for other craftspeople as a sub-contractor, thus at least utilising your talents and workspace, not to mention improving your skills with someone else's materials. Secondly, you could try to get any other part-time work at all: you would not be the first talented craftsperson to work behind a bar or wash dishes in order to pay the rent on a workshop. The third option is to teach at a school, a college or an evening class. Unless you already have teaching experience or good contacts in the academic world, you will find that teaching is unquestionably going to be the hardest not only to get into but also to do.

Nevertheless, unless you have the survival instincts of a lemming, you should be able to keep going somehow, until you have developed your dream into a viable business.

III
SELLING YOUR WORK

13
Pricing Your Product

This is probably the most vital section of the book, and if you are to succeed in business as a craftsperson, pricing should be your most important consideration when it comes to selling your product.

If you pitch your prices too high, you will have difficulty in selling your work. If your prices are too low, you reduce your profit margins. You also risk falling prey to the popular misconception that if something is too cheap it is of no value and not worth buying. The obvious middle path, of setting the price correctly, should give you a better chance of successfully selling your products and at the same time making a reasonable profit for yourself.

In order to arrive at a reasonably correct price structure for your products, you should consider the cost of your raw materials, consumables, overheads, labour, setting up and printing and packaging (if required). That at any rate is the theoretical method of pricing your work. However, you will probably find that you have calculated such a high price that unless you intend to produce very expensive 'one-offs', you will find it difficult to sell enough of your work to make it worth your while. If, on the other hand, you hope to sell lots of items (even one-offs) at a realistic price, you should review the aforementioned list and reconsider your calculations in a thoroughly businesslike manner. Thus the practical way of working out your prices should take into account the following:

Raw materials Purchase at the cheapest price (trade, bulk, wholesale), but do not sacrifice quality for cost.

Consumables These are the disposable items used in the

manufacturing process (sandpaper, knife blades etc) – purchase at the cheapest price (trade, bulk, wholesale).

Overheads Don't forget to include an element of your overheads in your price structure. To assess your overhead costs in relation to the cost of production, you will have to work out your total annual overheads and divide that total by the number of weeks you propose to work annually. For the sake of argument, let us say fifty weeks (you deserve a fortnight's break). Thus:

Rent	£1,200
Rates	£300
Electricity	£100
Fairs	£550
Vehicle and Travel	£1,000
Telephone	£160
Insurance	£140
Professional fees (accountant etc)	£120
Miscellaneous (leasing, interest payments)	£1,500
Total annual overheads	£5,070

In this example of a craft workshop whose owner travels to fairs, we find that the annual cost of maintaining the business (excluding direct manufacturing costs) is £5,070. We shall assume that the craftsperson is dedicated and works a fifty week year. Therefore, to find the aggregate weekly overheads bill, we simply divide the annual overheads by the number of working weeks: £5,070 ÷ 50 = £101.40. From the weekly rate, we can extract the hourly rate by working out, a) how many hours per week will be spent at work, and b) what proportion of those working hours will be spent actually manufacturing, as opposed to marketing, administration and travel.

Let us assume an eight hour working day, six-day week, which equals a forty-eight hour week; if only half that time is spent in manufacturing (which is not unusual), divide the hours per week by 50%: 48hrs/wk ÷ 50% = 24hrs/wk.

Finally, to find the aggregate hourly overheads rate in relation to production, divide the weekly cost by the time spent in manufacture: £101.40 ÷ 24 hrs/wk = £4.23.

Labour (manhours)   This is the relationship between the time spent in manufacturing and the amount you wish to earn per hour. When you calculate the cost of labour, it would be wise to consider that most craftspeople, regardless of what they produce, rarely earn more than £3 per hour for labour. Many craftspeople earn rather less. This is due mainly to the fact that highly skilled craftwork is by definition labour-intensive.

You will almost certainly find that, with practice, the time it takes you to produce your work will be drastically cut as you become more proficient, thereby reducing the cost of manhours/item accordingly, at which point you will benefit by an increased profit margin should you decide to maintain your prices at their original levels. If I am not the first to tell you, then at least let this be a confirmation that, in the unfair world in which we live, skilled craftspeople rarely, if ever, earn as much per hour as plumbers or electricians. Thus the idea of costing your labour at £15 or £20 per hour is somewhat unrealistic. However, if you set yourself a nominal target for annual earnings, of say £7,000, you should be able to calculate a labour rate to suit yourself.

Setting up   You should allow the cost of setting up, jigging up or preparing your screens (depending on what craft you practise) to be absorbed by the number of items you anticipate producing, otherwise you will find that your prices will be unrealistically high.

Printing and packaging   Bear in mind that the greater the print-run, the lower the cost per individual item.

Your pricing should now look a little more acceptable – if not to you, then at least to the buying public, whilst still allowing you to create your product at a profit that you should be able to live on.

To see how everything should come together, let us look at a typical costing for a product. For the purposes of this example we will use the overhead cost of £4.23 per hour already arrived at. The labour cost will be £3 per hour and the time needed to produce one item will be 2½ hours:

Materials	£2.30
Consumables	£0.50
Overheads	£10.58
Labour @ £3/hour	£7.50
Setting-up costs	£0.15
Total	£21.03

Having arrived at the basic manufacturing cost, you should look at it critically to see whether it is a realistic price in relation not only to your own profit margins but also to current market prices. There is no problem whatsoever if the manufacturing price is too low (though you had better check that you haven't made a mistake), but if, as is usually the case, the price you arrive at is too high for the market to bear, you will have to re-examine every single step of your manufacturing process and cut out wastage in both time and materials in order to reduce the overall cost.

When you are satisfied with the basic manufacturing price, you will be able to fine-tune the selling price to meet your own marketing stratagem.

For direct sales you should add ten or twenty per cent (more if you can) to the basic price to allow for a profit-margin above and beyond the element of labour costs.

When you sell to trade, bear in mind that retailers will double (at least) the price they pay you when they resell your product. This will have a considerable bearing on how they look on your work. For example, if the cheapest price you can make and sell a rocking horse for is £350, it will have a retail price of £700 in a toyshop, and trade buyers will need to judge whether they will be able to re-sell it at that price. While you should still add your profit margin, if you make allowances for the increased turnover that usually derives from trade sales, the percentage surcharge might be somewhat lower.

You will probably have to calculate your costings several times before you arrive at your final figure. Always temper your judgement with lashings of common sense, and on no account be totally governed by cold arithmetic if your common sense tells you otherwise. Before you decide on your final figure, have a look at the competition in shops, galleries and craft markets, or wherever else you may find work of a similar nature to your own. Take note of what the market will bear in relation to prices. Do not be too disheartened if at first you find you cannot bring your own prices in line with other people's, because it is only to provide you with a rule of thumb. Everything is subjective, even setting out your price structure.

Finally, two mutually contradictory pieces of conventional wisdom that apply to all aspects of pricing your product. The first I have already mentioned: the public often consider that if something is too cheap it is not worth buying – so don't sell yourself short. The second is that you should always bear in mind that 'Five per cent of something is better than a hundred per cent of nothing.' In other words, use your judgement not to price yourself out of the market.

14
Customers

There will be many occasions when you will feel that selling crafts would be pure pleasure if it weren't for customers getting in the way. Sad as it is, you are going to have to learn how to deal with them.

Many craftspeople have a natural ability to sell; others have to develop their own techniques for dealing with customers, or delegate the job to somebody else.

In the same way that I would not – or, more accurately, could not – dictate hard-and-fast rules on how to make crafts, neither can I lay down rules for being an ace salesperson. You should make your style a very personal one. If your approach is somewhat shy or alternatively a bit rough-hewn, don't worry about it. The important thing, as they say in advertising, is to be sincere, whether you mean it or not.

If it is any consolation to you, the customer is not always right; in fact, customers are seldom right. But it doesn't hurt to let them think they are right from time to time, especially when you are involved in the world of crafts. So much of the business of buying and selling craft items is tied up with intangible factors like taste and fashion, to say nothing of aesthetic values and traditional folk-memories, and when you try to sell something, you will unconsciously be operating on various psychological levels, not least of which is that of emotion.

Try to get the customers on your side, empathise with them and try to find out what they are looking for in your work. The responses can sometimes be quite illuminating.

It is not a bad idea to keep a record of all your customers' names and addresses. Very soon you will have a mailing list of people who may be interested in buying from you again, should you bring out a new range of products.

Keep your customers interested in your work. People quite often like to feel that they are involved in creative enterprises. You might consider inviting a selection of your best customers to a private viewing of your new season's work at your shop or workshop. For the cost of a few bottles of sale-or-return plonk and the loan of some glasses from the off-licence, you will flatter your existing customers by showing that you remembered to invite them, and probably sell a few items during the course of the preview. If you are particularly sneaky, you might even contact your local paper, regional arts magazine, radio and television stations and wangle a nice little editorial feature out of them (remember to invite the features editor).

Listen to what your customers have to say about your work. Nine times out of ten you won't agree with their views, but occasionally one of them will come up with a truly good idea that will be worth following up. Retaining your artistic integrity is all right if you are in a position to afford it, but most of us have to maintain a somewhat more pragmatic approach to our work. It is funny how, apropos of a casual remark from a browsing customer, you may be successful in landing a one-off commission or perhaps get the idea to produce a whole new range of items for a sector of the market that before you did not know existed.

Not surprisingly, there is a vast difference between dealing with trade customers and the buying-public. Trade buyers tend to take a fairly positive, no-nonsense line in deciding whether or not to buy from you. In the final analysis the deciding factor must be whether or not they feel they will be able to re-sell your work. The public generally like nothing better than a good 'dither'. Regardless of what the final outcome will be, the average customer will agonise, seemingly for hours, over colourways, sizes and goodness knows what else. How you deal with trade and public is a purely personal matter. Many craftspeople I know take great pleasure in playing a difficult customer, much as a skilled angler would tackle a prize salmon, whilst others prefer to deal only with professional buyers, with whom they feel they speak the same language.

Finally, never sell yourself short when dealing with a customer. If you are positive in your attitude towards your work, some of your enthusiasm may rub off on your customers. On the other hand, you must know when to keep quiet. Nothing can kill a sale stone-dead more than an over-effusive pushy sales pitch.

After a hard day at the shop or market stall it may be difficult to remember that customers are, after all, only human. Nevertheless, it is a sobering thought that, whatever you may think of your customers, none of us could survive without them. In the end it is they who will decide whether or not you succeed in business.

15
Window Display

Whilst this chapter is concerned mainly with shop window display, there is no reason why it cannot also apply to the arrangement of exhibits at craft fairs.

It should not be necessary to remind you that the primary function of display is to help you sell your merchandise. The general standard of window display in Britain is depressingly dreary. Craft shops are no exception, which is surprising since the whole ethos of crafts is closely related to design and flair. Display is too frequently treated as an afterthought, which is a shame as it is probably the first thing the customer sees. If you give some thought to dressing your window, you will be rewarded by the interest it will generate.

The finest practitioners of the art of window-dressing are major department stores. They became aware very early on of the value of an effective display and devote considerable money and time to creating windows that appear effortlessly to present the promise of what lies within.

Take a stroll along the main shopping thoroughfares. See how the different stores create their individual effects. For an example of imaginative display, look at Liberty's or Jaeger's windows in London's Regent Street. Harvey Nichols' windows in Sloane Street are nearly always dramatically stark, and yet with a minimum of merchandise they manage to say a great deal about the overall style of the store. As distinct from the artfully contrived display, Habitat's windows merge so effortlessly into the character of the selling-area that you can be almost unaware of their presence. But make no mistake: that too is intentional, because it helps to eliminate the barrier between the street and

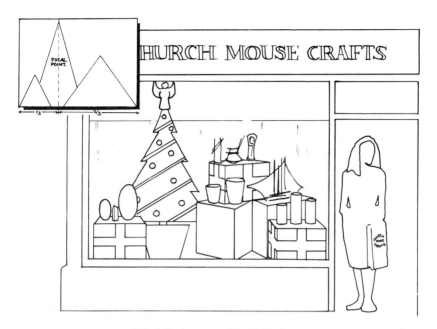

Fig 2 An 'asymmetrical' display

the store. Fashion shops have the most scope for exciting displays, and though certain shops tend to go in and out of favour, the Next chain has created a recognisable house-style that is worth looking at.

Take into account the visual aspect of what you are displaying in the window. Group items together on different visual levels. Place small items where they will be seen to the greatest advantage. Keep a sense of order in your display; don't fall into the trap of overloading the window with little bits and pieces of everything in the shop. It doesn't take much to make a display look untidy.

Be daring and witty. One of the most effective window displays I can remember was in Tommy Nutter's shop, where he showed his expensive suits in dustbins. This was all the more remarkable because it was in Savile Row, where one doesn't expect such flippancy.

It is usually best to use adjustable overhead-track **lighting**, if for no other reason than that people expect to see light coming down (the sun in the sky, etc). By using overhead illumination, you will keep hot bulbs as far away from the display as possible, thus avoiding potential damage.

If you want to introduce a more dramatic effect, you can play with floor-mounted lights or coloured bulbs and filters. However, with coloured lighting you risk altering the colours or tones of the items displayed (fine with glass or crystal, not so fine with clothing).

Regarding **colour**, we are no longer bound by the clichés of navy-blue/white for spring; blue/yellow for summer; rust/green for autumn; red/green for Christmas. Nevertheless, a thoughtfully colour-co-ordinated display will give a far stronger, more cohesive window with added visual impact.

If you have a space to fill with a display, you should arrange it so there is a definite focal point. The simplest and most effective way of achieving this effect is to create an **asymmetrical display**. This involves placing the focal point one-third in from one side (see Fig 2). By so doing you will be able to create an interesting display with great depth.

Experiment with different types of display, changing them periodically. But whatever else, please give your display the care and thought that your stock deserves.

16
Marketing

Now is the time to consider how to set about marketing (technical jargon for selling) your work. Of the various options open to you, we shall consider the three most basic methods of shifting your crafts onto an unsuspecting public. These methods, when reduced to their simplest forms, fall into two distinct categories: direct and trade. Depending on your situation and aptitude, you should decide whether to opt for one or the other or both of these methods.

DIRECT SALES

Direct selling is more than just retailing, for it is exactly what its name implies, in that you, the craftsperson, sell your product directly to the customer without anyone in the middle taking their cut or adding on their mark-up. The positive side of direct sales is that you will receive more money per item sold, because in effect you will be setting your own recommended retail price to suit yourself. You will have the pleasure of meeting the public and quite often be able to share their enthusiasm for what you make. You will certainly have greater control over what you make, which for most of us is what being a craftsperson is all about.

On the other hand, you will have to find the time to deal with the public, regardless of whether it be at craftmarkets, fairs, their premises or your own. Time is an expensive commodity for a small business.

Peter and Lucy are silversmiths. They started by selling their work from a stall at a large and currently fashionable craft market.

Originally they both taught part-time. They made their stock on their days off and in the evenings, and every Saturday and Sunday, regardless of the weather, they set up their stall in the market. Their regular attendance gave them a kind of permanence, and the public soon came to know where to find them in the market. Before long Peter and Lucy had built up a solid clientele. After a few years of operating in this way, they felt secure enough to concentrate on their craftwork and began to phase out their teaching altogether.

Apart from the fact that they enjoy dealing with the public, neither Peter nor Lucy feels they have the time or ability to deal with retailers – besides which they would find it hard to bring their costs down to a mutually acceptable wholesale price. Eventually they hope to move out of the market and open up a shop of their own. Until that happens they feel that the relative simplicity of their present set-up suits them just fine.

Other than in exceptional circumstances, direct selling, by its very nature, restricts you to selling one item per customer, often without the opportunity of repeat orders. If you decide to sell at craft fairs, you must remember to work out the costs of space, petrol etc and try to accommodate them into your pricing structure.

TRADE (WHOLESALE) SALES

As its name suggests, a trade sale means that you sell your work to a retailer, who will usually double the price they paid you and hope to resell your product to the public. Don't make the mistake of begrudging shopkeepers their mark-ups, because they have to take the risk that what they have bought from you may stay on their shelves for months on end.

As opposed to direct sales, and in order to allow a decent retail mark-up, you may find that you receive less money per individual item that you sell; however, you can expect to sell considerably more items per customer. If your product sells successfully, you will probably also benefit by getting repeat orders from the shops.

Angela produces her own screen-printed textiles from her workshop in the village where she now lives, after moving out of

London. The financial incentives and the price of property convinced her that her decision to move had been the right one. Very soon she had developed a network of homeworkers from the villagers to manufacture her prints into a range of giftware.

Due to the remoteness of her village, Angela has had to rely on selling her work to retailers in order to maintain the sales turnover necessary for her survival.

After a couple of years of trial and error she found that, if she exhibited her range at four of the major gift fairs throughout the year, more than enough business would be generated to keep her and her workforce busy all year round.

The other main benefit of running a business along these lines is that very little is made speculatively. Production can be planned two or three months in advance, and purchasing and cashflow can be arranged accordingly.

Angela is the first to admit that she has been extraordinarily lucky in the way things have worked out for her. She could just as easily not have found the right market for her product, and as such she would have been stranded in her lovely village with no customers and no orders. As it is, she has a lively business. She is bringing employment to her community, and she is able to live and work in a place of her choice.

As mentioned in chapter 13, the most straightforward and generally accepted percentage mark-up from trade price to retail is one hundred per cent. It will be in your best interest, if you sell direct and trade not to undercut the shops whom you supply when you make a direct sale to a member of the public. You will soon find out, if you didn't already know, that the craftworld is terribly small, as word will get back to the shopkeeper, who will quite rightly feel somewhat peeved (or worse) and may with some justification decide to stop buying from you.

The most common exception to the one hundred per cent mark-up is when you sell through a gallery or at an exhibition. In these cases it is accepted practice for the gallery to take a thirty per cent (at least) commission from the selling price. However, in the end it is up to you to negotiate the most advantageous deal.

Marketing

SALE OR RETURN
From time to time retailers may ask you to supply them on a sale or return basis, which means that if the items are not sold they will be returned to you. Other than in exceptional circumstances, you should refuse such offers. The retailers who operate a SOR scheme are usually taking advantage of the inexperienced craftsperson. It is a way to stock their shop for little or no capital outlay and at no risk to themselves. Should you nevertheless decide to agree to supply a shop on a SOR basis, perhaps as a way of introducing your work onto their shelves, I suggest that you agree on a time limit for your work to stay there. Otherwise you may end up committing a lot of your work to a shop that, for whatever reason, is not selling it and therefore not earning you any money, and a year later receiving back a lot of old stock. Very few craftspeople can afford to let stock be tied up in this way and I imagine that you will be no exception.

MAIL ORDER
For many craftspeople mail-order selling combines the best of all possible worlds especially if you are based far away from what passes for civilisation. Your main problem is going to be persuading the erstwhile buying public not only that you exist but also that you have a terrific product to sell.

The obvious solution is to advertise (dealt with in chapter 19). Bear in mind that most worthwhile advertising will not be cheap, but you may find that the costs of advertising and all the expenses entailed are more than offset by the pleasure of being able to work undisturbed in your rural idyll.

If in the course of your business you invite consumers to place pre-paid orders for goods to be despatched by post, you will be liable to the Mail Order Transaction (Information) Order 1976. Under this order you will be required to include in 'legible characters' your true (or registered business) name and the address at which the business is managed on all communications, ie advertisements, catalogues, circulars, invitations (express or implied) to consumers to order the goods described therein, or communications stating or inferring that payment is to be made before the goods are despatched.

If you ring up the Postal Representatives Department at your local post office, they will be delighted to make an appointment to chat to you about the wonderful mysteries of COD (Cash On Delivery), Freepost, Reply Paid and Mailshot. And believe me, sometimes the ways of the post office can be mysterious indeed. The post office will also arrange to collect outgoing mail from your premises if you regularly despatch large quantities.

You might also use companies like Securicor, which offers a competitive nationwide door-to-door delivery service for parcels and packets. Provided that you get your message across to the public, mail-order sales can offer you the freedom to work and live wherever you want, and also to take advantage of inexpensive premises, by not having to be in a good shopping district.

17
Fairs and Markets

When you are starting out, you will find that the simplest, cheapest and most effective way of obtaining the exposure your product deserves is to sell at craft fairs and markets.

You will soon discover that there are clearly defined circuits for the specialist craft fairs (dolls and dolls' houses, for example) and also for those of a more general craft nature. If you have the time and inclination, it might not be a bad idea to spend a year or so 'doing' the fair circuit and getting yourself known by the public. In that time you should also have the opportunity of being noticed by the press who attend craft fairs, thereby acquiring some publicity.

Generally speaking, taking a stall at a craft fair or market is a relatively inexpensive way of direct selling, when you consider that the organisers of a well-run event will almost certainly have undertaken to generate considerable local interest, through advertising and the press, thus leaving to you the chore of prising money out of the customers.

Visitors to craft fairs and markets are, generally speaking, a well-ordered bunch who possess a genuine appreciation for crafts and craftsmanship. If there is one failing that they are prone to it is the jumble-sale mentality, usually accentuated when a fair is held in a church hall. The symptoms consist of the assumption that they will find a bargain on your stall, which then turns to slightly grumpy resentment when you insist on selling your work for a profit. There is no known cure for this tragic inability to differentiate between jumble sales, sales of work and craft fairs, but with good humour and a lot of patience we can at least alleviate their disappointment.

All craft events, whether fairs or markets, will provide you with a marvellous opportunity to escape from the confinement of your workshop or studio and see what is happening in the world outside. You will also have the chance to meet other craftspeople, compare work and techniques and exchange ideas with them. Strange as it may seem, you should find that the majority of craftspeople are happy to share their knowledge with you, provided you are not going to use that knowledge to rip them off. Indeed, I have noticed that the more skilled the craftsperson, the more they are prepared to help the newcomer. Conversely, the less able craftsperson often goes to extraordinary lengths to safeguard 'trade secrets' that are ninety-nine per cent hogwash.

When you decide to attend a fair, give some thought to the overall costs that will be involved, especially if the event lasts for more than one day or if you are accompanied by a helper. Let us look at the costs of a craftsperson from out of town who participating in a relatively inexpensive three day fair in central London in 1985. These costs are fairly typical as the bare minimum that you can expect to pay for any major event that takes place away from your home town:

Space (6 x 4ft)	£75.00
Display	£40.00
Printing (brochures, price lists, etc)	£60.00
Hotel for three nights (for one person)	£85.00
Travel (return)	£35.00
Miscellaneous (food etc)	£100.00
Total	£395.00

This craftsperson was sensible enough to have worked out the probable cost beforehand and was therefore able to plan accordingly. Prices were fixed to accommodate the overheads, and sufficient stock was brought to justify the capital outlay. At the end of the fair over £900 worth of stock had been sold 'over the counter' and a further £3,000 worth of orders had been placed for delivery within two months – a relatively profitable three days.

That example is conservative in the extreme. Most fairs will be considerably more expensive, and some will be of longer duration. You may even have to pay extra for the use of electricity or lighting supplied to your stand. Nevertheless it illustrates how, without undue extravagance, a £75 stand can end up costing £400, added to which you should bear in mind that, if you work on your own, you will have lost at least five days' production by attending the fair. (One day for travelling and setting up, one day for dismantling and returning the stock to your workshop, and three days selling.)

You will have to regard all these costs in terms of overheads, much in the same way as a shopkeeper would consider rent on a shop. As such they should be taken into consideration when you price your product.

Organise yourself before you set off for the fair. Make certain you have coloured pens (for writing signs), Sellotape, double-sided tape, little sticky labels for writing prices on, staples in your staple gun, drawing-pins, hammer, screwdriver, Stanley knife, spare bulbs for spotlights, extension cable, felt, tablecloths, lots of Blu-Tack (without which we should all fall apart) and boxes to carry everything in. Bear in mind that wherever you are, you are going to be miles from shops that will be open, especially on a Sunday. So, short of oxygen and pitons, prepare yourself for every eventuality, because, as we all know, whatever can go wrong will.

Ensure that you have packed sufficient stock, and consider how you will display it on your stall. A bright, welcoming and above all interesting stand is bound to attract more potential customers than one that looks a mess.

If you propose selling regularly at fairs or markets, you may decide to build or buy some easily transportable 'knock-down' shelving or screens for your display. Alternatively you can produce an interesting effect by placing different-sized boxes under a tablecloth to create small display areas on different levels. Look at how other craftspeople manage to create interesting and inviting layouts on their stands, and try to emulate (but never copy) them. Load your stall with merchandise if you must, but try to avoid creating a messy environment, because it will only tend to confuse the public, who will simply walk on to the next stall and ignore yours completely.

If you are selling jewellery or clothing, remember to incorporate a mirror in your display so that people can see for themselves how terrific they look wearing your work.

Give yourself plenty of time to plan how you are going to arrange your display. Contact the organisers of the event and ascertain the exact dimensions of the space they have allocated to you. Find out if there are any rear or dividing walls on your stand and, if so, what they are made of. You might wish to screw in some shelving, which would be impossible on, for example, a canvas divider. Finally find out whether the organisers will supply tables and/or chairs for you to use on your stand.

Try to get a corner site if you can, because it will allow you to double your display frontage. At all costs avoid being located halfway down an aisle that is a cul-de-sac, because the public seem to have an aversion to walking into dead ends. Check whether there will be electricity on, or near, your stand, and make provision for extra spotlights, in case the lighting level in the hall is inadequate.

Far be it from me to tell you how to design your stand. Let me simply say that the two basic configurations for fair or market stalls can best be described as 'internal' and 'external'.

The internal display (see Fig 3) allows the customer to come inside your display area to browse and be served. This design is particularly suited to products that require wallspace (pictures, wall-hangings, etc) or floorspace (rocking horses, furniture, etc). The external display (see Fig 4) is more like a shop counter, the table acting as a barricade between you and the public. This is the easiest and quickest display to mount at short notice and is

Fig 3 An 'internal' display

Fig 4 An 'external' display

Fig 5 A variation on an 'external' display

especially suited for small, valuable items that require constant vigilance against the 'light-fingered brigade'. A variation of the external display is when the stallholder comes round to the front of the stand (see Fig 5), allowing greater scope in creating an interesting backdrop display at the rear of the table.

Graphic displays are usually most effective when simple and in keeping with your product. Their job is to attract the customers to your stand but not to distract them from the merchandise.

A good way of attracting the public is by putting on a demonstration of your craft. The British – and, for all I know, the whole of humanity – like nothing better than to watch other people at work. They will cluster round your stand, ask you silly questions and generally be a nuisance, but the main thing is that, whilst you have got their attention, you also have the opportunity to make a sale. Sneaky, huh?

Always have a pile of business cards or handbills at the front of your stall, so that people may easily pick them up. Very often, perhaps months after having seen you at a fair, someone may contact you to order a special birthday or Christmas present purely on the strength of having picked up one of your cards. If you have gone to the trouble and, more importantly, the expense of printing brochures or catalogues, you should display only a few at a time, since, given the opportunity, the public will blithely pick them up and throw them away, often without even bothering to read them. If you restrict your literature to people who specifically ask, you will not be wasting it.

Very often price will be a major factor in your success at fairs. It will come as no surprise to learn that stallholders who have items selling at £1 or less will usually be much busier than those with a stall full of expensive collectable crafts. Don't let this discourage you, should you fall into the latter category. In fact, let it work to your advantage by having a tray of less expensive gewgaws on your stall to tempt customers and engage their interest. If you are a potter or a ceramicist, you may decide to have a selection of seconds or rejects, which, believe it or not, people will be delighted to buy at a slightly reduced price.

Take a lesson from the supermarkets, which are nothing if not professional in the art (or science) of selling. Play the customers at their own game by lopping 5p off a nice round pound figure. The majority of customers seem to possess built-in price barriers. By pitching your price just below their cut-off point you will stand a much better chance of making a sale.

Many established markets have regular stallholders, and you will find that there is a waiting-list for stalls. However, if you are determined enough to turn up very early in the morning, you may be able to occupy the stall of a regular who has not shown up that day. This constitutes a 'casual' stall. If you succeed in being a casual often enough, you can then be accepted as a 'regular' yourself, although in some of the more popular markets you will probably be collecting your pension before that happens. It is a risky exercise but in the case of markets like Covent Garden and Jubilee Market it is well worth it.

You will find that outdoor craft markets have a sub-culture all their own. If you are a masochist, you will enjoy yourself immensely, especially towards Christmas. Never on any account leave home without your leg-warmers and layers of woolly clothing. It doesn't matter how daft you look provided you are warm and dry.

I should warn you about participating at 'craft fayres'. I don't know why but 'fayres', as opposed to 'fairs', are usually a dead loss. I suspect that it is the overall tweeness of trying to be olde worlde, but it just never seems to work. People who organise 'craft fayres' tend to be well-meaning but not very professional.

Over the past few years there has been a remarkable proliferation of craft fairs and events all over the country. Some will be well organised and profitable; others will be such a total waste of time and money that they won't even be an educational experience.

I could not adequately list or categorise all the craft fairs that exist. However, I have listed the five major venues for high-quality contemporary British crafts that are generally considered the top, most prestigious events in the craft calendar.

As a rule you will find that as a prospective exhibitor at any of the top events you will have to apply to the organisers as much as nine months to a year in advance. The organisers will usually then select the exhibitors from among the applicants. The competition for space at fairs like those listed below is quite fierce, and though the prestigious and better-known fairs tend to be fairly expensive, you should offset the cost against the opportunity for increased sales.

Art In Action, Waterperry House, near Wheatley, Oxford. Date: July. A four-day event covering the whole spectrum of fine arts and crafts, set in the famous gardens of Waterperry House. There are craft demonstrations, practical classes, concerts and a craft market.
Contact for further details: 96 Sedlescombe Road, London SW6 1RB (01-381 3192).

Craft Fair Chelsea, Chelsea Old Town Hall, Kings Road, London SW3. Date: October. This is an established, highly prestigious, generally well-organised fair encompassing all crafts. Open to the public, it is usually highly profitable for exhibitors, due to early Christmas shoppers. The fair is usually about a week long but exhibitors can take split weeks.

Contact for further details: 16 The Little Boltons, London SW10.

Festival Crafts Fair, West Princes Street, Edinburgh. Date: August. A highly-thought-of craft event, timed to coincide with the Edinburgh Festival. The fair lasts ten days and features some of the most exciting contemporary British crafts.

Contact for further details: Lindean Mill Glass, Lindean Mill, Galashiels, Selkirkshire.

Harrogate Craft Trade Fair. Date: May. Trade buyers only. This is an excellent venue for craftspeople wishing to sell to retailers. It is usually very difficult to get space at Harrogate but you could try to get in at short notice if somebody cancels their allocation.

Contact for further details: PKD Ltd, Mill Green, Waterside, Colne, Lancs (Colne 867153).

Top Drawer, Kensington Exhibition Centre, Derry Street, London W8. Date: April and September. Trade buyers only. A prestigious giftware trade fair. Strictly speaking, exhibits are not restricted solely to crafts, and over the past few years there has tended to be an emphasis on clothing and fashion; however, the accent is definitely on quality products.

Contact for further details: Dresswell Exhibitions Ltd, Blenheim House, 137 Blenheim Crescent, London W11 2EQ (01-727 1929).

Don't allow yourself to be disheartened should your work be rejected by the organisers of any fair. Remember that selection committees are subjective and idiosyncratic in their choice.

Lastly, I speak for thousands of craftspeople up and down the country who have suffered by pitching a stall next to someone who makes musical or irritatingly noisy objects. Please, please don't demonstrate them interminably.

18
Export

This is the big one. Crack the export market and you should have it made. Most established craftspeople regard the export market, especially the USA, as their main source of income, and for many of them it constitutes over ninety per cent of orders.

It is, in a modest way, quite a success story in itself that worldwide demand for British craft products has been on the increase while larger industries have been taking a hammering. This is due almost entirely to the fact that over the past few years the quality of craftsmanship and design coming out of British workshops has been remarkably high. In the context of British crafts, 'Made In Britain' is seen by foreign buyers as a recommendation and not a criticism.

The best markets for British crafts at the moment are undoubtedly the USA (particularly California) and Japan (especially for dolls and extremely intricate items like dolls' house furniture). Surprisingly, France is a very good market for hand-made British products, even though they haven't forgiven us for Waterloo. Most craftspeople thrive on exporting, and it is probably easier to find high-quality British crafts in California or Texas than in Britain itself. The key to this renaissance of British crafts is that we are managing to produce hand-made, high-quality goods at a time when most of the world is turning to high technology. Admittedly we are restricted predominantly to the luxury markets, but if that is what is available to us, let's take advantage of it.

Some people depend totally on their export sales and make the mistake of taking them for granted. This assumption can land one in a terrible mess because of the multitude of factors that affect every aspect of exporting, from the rate of the dollar to changing tariffs, not to mention the occasional war or *coup d'état*.

The main drawback to selling abroad is that everywhere is such a long way away (relatively speaking). If you are a small business, you are bound to find it difficult to take orders, contact customers or nag for payment halfway across the world. The solution to that problem is to find an agent who will represent your interests in whatever country you choose to export to. Apart from anything else, an agent will speak the local language and understand the niceties of local business practice. You may decide to appoint a friend or relative to be your agent, or you may use a professional agent. It doesn't matter who represents you so long as they produce results. Above all else, however, you must find an agent (see chapter 20) whom you can trust totally to promote your interests and look after your money.

The British Overseas Trade Board is a section of the Department of Trade & Industry. Its headquarters are at 1 Victoria Street, London SW1H 0ET, with ten regional offices throughout the UK. The Board offers practical help to exporters: financial assistance for British manufacturers to exhibit at overseas trade fairs, and foreign visits to explore potential export markets. Apart from financial help, the BOTB also provides specific information about overseas markets and foreign competition. It will also try to arrange introductions between exporters and potential customers.

It publishes a wide selection of useful booklets that cover all aspects of exporting, from the general information contained in the *Export Handbook* (HMSO) to the series *Hints to Exporters*.

When you receive an export order from a new customer, you probably won't know how good they are going to be at paying you. You would be well advised to safeguard your interests by issuing a pro-forma invoice (see chapter 21) before you despatch the goods. This precaution is not because of the untrustworthy nature of foreigners (Good Heavens, some of my best customers are foreigners) but merely because it is a very long way to travel to collect a bad debt.

If you need more substantial assurances, you should contact the Export Credit Guarantee Department, PO Box 272, Aldermanbury House, Aldermanbury Square, London EC2P 2EL (01-606 6699). The ECGD helps exporters by insuring exporting companies against non-payment by their foreign customers, and by providing guarantees to the exporter's bank in order to facilitate finance for export business.

If you wish to cover yourself against currency fluctuations or bank commission rates if you are paid in foreign currency, you may decide to prepare a price list specifically for export, pitched about eight to ten per cent above your home prices. This is a matter that you must decide after you have taken into account how much export business you are transacting.

Take out adequate insurance for your product, especially if you export to the USA. You must cover yourself for public liability for at least £250,000, if not more, to protect yourself against litigious Americans. You should also consider taking out insurance for 'goods in transit' because in the long run it will be cheaper than registration or compensation insurance from the Post Office. You should always quote realistic delivery dates and try to keep to them. Nothing gives an exporter a bad name like late deliveries.

Ensure that you complete all the necessary documentation and customs dockets for the country concerned. If you are in any doubt, you should contact your local Customs and Excise office, post office or SITPRO. SITPRO stands for 'Simplification of International Trade Procedures Board', and its brief is to 'rationalise international trade procedures and documentation'. Apart from information, you will be able to purchase 'Postpacks', which are documentation sets for postal exports. Further information about SITPRO can be obtained from Almack House, 26–8 King Street, London SW1Y 6QW (01-214 3399). Try to do everything within your power to minimise any delays that might occur.

Always bear in mind that, as a rule, foreigners do not share our sense of humour. Try not to jeopardise a sale by being witty.

19
Advertising and Publicity

The obvious way of obtaining popular recognition of your work is by exploiting the news media as much as you can. In this chapter we shall explore the ways in which advertising can help you and, most important of all, how you can help yourself to advertising.

There are three basic methods for getting publicity. One method will cost as much, or as little, as you can afford. The second can be even more expensive than the first, whereas, for no more than the cost of a stamp or a telephone call, the last option is probably the most effective.

Should you decide to place an advertisement in a newspaper or journal, you will have to pay for the space and also supply 'print-ready' artwork, which may or may not cost you a lot, depending on whether you can wield pen, ink and Letraset yourself or must pay a graphic artist to do this for you.

It will come as no surprise to learn that each newspaper has its own rates for advertising, usually calculated on the size of its distribution area and audited readership. In other words, a popular national newspaper will charge considerably more per column inch than your local rag.

If you want to advertise, you must decide at the outset:

● How much you can afford to spend.
● How much you can realistically recoup through sales.
● Can you cope with an overwhelming response? (It might happen.)

Carefully target potential customers by advertising your

product in special-interest magazines that collectors of your particular craft will buy. Above all, use your resources as sparingly and as thoughtfully as you can, because an advertising campaign, however small, can swallow up your money without any difficulty whatever. In fact, it is a good idea to decide on an advertising budget at the outset, and not spend anything above that limit without very good cause indeed.

If you have done your research properly, and that includes the vital aspect of design and layout of the actual advertisement, you will stand a much better chance of selling your work. Be careful, however, that the cost of your advertising campaign does not wipe out the chance of any profit that you make from your sales. You will have no way of assessing this problem, but it is often the case and should be borne in mind.

Jonathan is a cabinet-maker. He soon realised that personal recommendation from satisfied customers was not enough to maintain the momentum of orders necessary to keep him busy. He needed to advertise simply to make the public aware of his company's existence.

The first thing he had to do was to analyse his potential market. He then targeted the type of customer he wanted to reach, and the geographical area he could cover. Because he was London-based, Jonathan decided to concentrate on London and the Home Counties. Initially he began to advertise in the local press. This, added to one or two editorial features, generated a lot of interest and a few orders which he would not have got otherwise. He then took advantage of a special offer and placed £200 worth of advertising in *City Limits*, which brought in orders worth £20,000 (over a period of a year or more). This seemed to show him the direction to take, and he decided to concentrate his publicity campaign accordingly. He decided to go upmarket and began regularly taking out quarter-page advertisements in the glossies (*Homes & Gardens, House & Garden, Ideal Home* etc).

Jonathan keeps his publicity and advertising under constant review. His budget falls just below the usually accepted ten per cent of turnover, but he feels that he has got the balance just about right for his business. Although he employs professional graphic designers and copywriters for his advertisements, he retains strict control over their work, because ultimately it is his reputation and company image they are playing with.

The direct results of Jonathan's present campaign are in line with the experience of other advertisers. One in twenty reader enquiries develops into a request for further information. Out of that one person in five will place a firm order. This response of one per cent is pretty average for a general broad-based advertising campaign.

As a final cautionary note on paid advertising, please remember to include your address and/or telephone number in the artwork. It may seem obvious to you now but you would be amazed how many advertisers assume that because they know their own address, everybody else does too. 'T'ain't so!

I won't waste much time on press agents and PROs, the second option available to you. This is not because they are not effective – they are in fact extremely effective – but because most craftspeople in a start-up situation are unable to afford their services. For a fee, your publicity person will assiduously promote your product (or, indeed, you, if you like) to the newspapers, radio, television and anybody who might be interested. The outcome of all this frenzy of activity will be that you should obtain lots of 'free' editorials.

By taking a bit of trouble and a lot of nerve, you should be able to achieve something similar by your own efforts. And who knows, your approach may have a freshness and appeal that the professionals lack (though to give them their due I doubt it).

Contrary to the conventional wisdom that 'nothing is for nothing', you will find that the most effective form of advertising for the craftsperson is the truly free editorial. People who disbelieve everything else that they read in their newspaper seem to trust implicitly articles that evaluate or criticise the Arts, New Products, Fashions and Design. More importantly, you will find that readers will often follow up an article by contacting you with an order or a request for further information.

Luck is going to play a large part in whether you get written up or not; so too will perseverance. Spend as much time as you can afford telephoning the features editor of every newspaper, TV and radio station you can think of. At this stage in the proceedings you needn't be too discriminating: use the telephone like scattershot. You will be rejected by some papers and accepted by others, but if you hadn't taken the trouble to call them, they would not have been aware of your existence.

An alternative variation of the above method, and one that usually gets better results, will be to send a press release together with some photographs (if you have any good ones) to all the papers, magazines, journals, radio stations and television programmes. Follow the mailshot up about a week later with your telephone call to the features editor. If they have read your press release, so much the better; if they have filed it in the waste bin, your call might refresh their memory and be enough for them to consider doing an article about you.

You'll find that, whereas newspapers can fit a feature article in at fairly short notice, the coloured glossies and colour supplements are usually planned four to six months in advance, so if you want publicity for a proposed exhibition or some other major event you will have to plan accordingly. When you prepare your press release, try to compose it in such a way that the editor can insert whole chunks of it into an article. Most editors are too busy to write all the articles that appear in their columns, so you will be doing everyone a favour if you can write your own article within the context of a press release. Take care with the presentation. Keep it concise and accessible. Type it, or have it set double-spaced on a sheet of good-quality A4 paper. The information should be bright and, if possible, related to something happening in the news either locally or nationwide. Insert all the relevant details about yourself and your product, and if you do hype it a bit no one is going to mind.

The following is an example of the type of layout you might try:

PRESS RELEASE
A Church Mouse Comes to Town

An exciting new shop has just opened at 25 The Shambles, Chipping-under-Water, Glos GL5 K9. **Church Mouse Crafts** produces a wide range of treen giftware made from exotic hardwoods. It offers a combination of originality of design and traditional skills rarely seen today.

The proprietor of Church Mouse Crafts is Bob Leonard. After a career in industry he decided to follow a dream. He started his own business two years ago in his garden shed. The business grew very quickly as his reputation for craftsmanship spread. And now, having outgrown the garden shed, he is moving into a shop in The Shambles.

Although Church Mouse Crafts is a fairly new arrival on the crafts scene, examples of its work are to be seen in the permanent collections of several museums (including the Watkins Collection). Bob was also a gold-medallist at the 1985 Berlin Kunstsalon for his centrepiece (later presented by the curator of the Salon to HSH Princess Charmian on the occasion of her wedding).

Visitors to the shop are welcome to visit the adjacent workshop in the newly restored Tudor cow-byre to see the products being made. They may also choose their own piece of timber from the wide range available, and see it turned into a thimble (or anything else from the list of designs) whilst they wait.

If you require further information or photographs, please contact: Florence, 01-234 5678.

I make no apologies for the deathless prose in the above example; generally that tends to be the format for most press releases.

Nevertheless, don't be tied by convention. If you think you can attract the attention of the press in any other way, give it a try. But unless you have got the personality to carry it off, don't go too far over the top with your press release because you will put everyone off and defeat the whole purpose of the exercise.

Try to keep a stock of photographs for publicity purposes. You will require very good, sharp colour transparencies and glossy black-and-white photographs of a similar high quality. If you are a good photographer so much the better; if not you should consider hiring a professional to photograph your work in a way that will do it justice.

If a newspaper or magazine requests photographic or graphic material from you, it will usually return it to you provided you write your name and address on the back of the artwork or on the frame.

You may find you will be approached by a local newspaper or magazine trying to sell advertising space. Remember that whoever is selling the space is in all likelihood a far better salesperson than you. This may of course be turned to your advantage by coming to an agreement whereby you take out an advertisement provided the paper will write about you in an editorial feature. A newspaper is usually quite happy to do this because it has not only sold some advertising but also filled in an empty space on the arts page. So, all things being equal, everyone should be satisfied.

Because of the proliferation of local newspapers, special-interest journals and radio stations, not to mention local news coverage on television, I doubt if it has ever been so easy to get publicity. But do not fall into the trap of believing your own hype: if you do, you will get yourself into the most awful pickle.

Right! That's sorted out fame. Now all we need to do is concentrate on riches . . .

20
Agents

There are many craftspeople who, for reasons of choice, geography or disposition, find it impossible to go out and sell the products they make. Fortunately for them, commerce, like nature, abhors a vacuum and there exist people of much hardier stock, called agents, whose sole aim in life is to sell the work of others.

From the point of view of most craftspeople, agents divide into two main groups: those that buy, and those that sell.

In the context of selling crafts, a **buying-agent** is one who acts for a store or group of stores, usually foreign, which retains its own representatives to work out of a British office for the express purpose of arranging and co-ordinating purchases from British sources.

An efficient buying operation will not only make introductions between the client company and the craftsperson but deal with all matters relating to the transaction, from the initial order to the collection and shipment, packaging and, in due course, the payment. The buying-agent will also be expected to keep abreast of any new products on the market that may be of interest to the client, and will devote a considerable amount of time and effort to visiting trade fairs and contacting potential new suppliers.

From your point of view, as a craftsperson who is approached by a buying agent, provided you can agree on a price and delivery date, the only thing left for you to do is to produce the goods to the same standard as your sample and, just as important, have them ready for collection or despatch on time. The client on whose behalf the buying-agent is acting should in most circumstances pay all the add-on charges, such as the agent's commission, freight costs, etc.

The British Overseas Trade Board at 1 Victoria Street, London SW1Y 0ET (01-215 7677), is generally helpful as a source of information about who represents which company and where their respective offices are. Later, when you are in a better position to prepare your marketing stratagem, you might consider compiling a list of buying-agents whom you can contact in the hope that they will be interested in what you produce.

Selling-agents, or representatives, represent you and your interests. It is their job to go out and contact new customers and pay courtesy calls on established clients. An agent will usually undertake to make sales, arrange demonstrations and collect payments on your behalf.

If you have not so far acquired the knack of being in three places at once (however hard you might have tried), you will soon discover the benefit of using an agent, especially when selling abroad. Having somebody representing you on the territory who speaks the language and understands local business etiquette, can prove invaluable, especially when customers need to be reminded about outstanding debts.

The way in which most craftspeople acquire their agents is best illustrated by the following example:

Jim was contacted by a chap he had met three weeks previously at a craft fair in Yorkshire where Jim had taken a stall. The prospective agent had seen Jim's work at the fair and felt that it was the sort of thing he could sell to the shops and stores he already supplied with craft and gift wares. He enquired whether Jim already had an agent.

'No,' said Jim. 'I've never felt I needed one. In any case, I sell all I want at craft fairs.'

To cut a long story short, they agreed that the agent should market Jim's products for a trial period of twelve months, at the end of which they would review the situation.

As things turned out, after the first year the agent had successfully sold Jim's work both at home and abroad, dealing with sectors of the market that, left to his own devices, Jim could never have reached. The result of this was that turnover and productivity increased beyond Jim's expectations. Needless to say, they agreed to continue the arrangement. All this was achieved without a written contract, just a mutual understanding that neither would do the dirty on the other.

Believe it or not, that is how most craftspeople acquire agents, and as long as the relationship depends in equal parts on trust and results, it seems to work pretty well.

Most agents with whom you will have dealings are self-employed. Some work full-time and are thoroughly professional in their approach, whilst others are agents in their spare time as an extension of their interest in (and sometimes passion for) crafts, and because it provides them with the opportunity of mixing in the world of crafts and craftspeople.

Provided the person whom you choose to represent you drums up enough business to suit your purposes, it doesn't really matter whether they are full-time, part-time, students or pensioners. Different craftspeople have differing expectations of success, and whereas some will feel the need to work for twenty-five hours a day, eight days a week, others will be more than happy to sell only as much as they care to produce, whilst still having time to relax with their families.

Trust will be a major consideration when dealing with any agent both at home and abroad. Bear in mind that your customers' attitude towards you and your product will be greatly influenced by the behaviour of your agent. If you feel that they cannot be relied on to represent your work as you would wish, forget it; choose someone in whom you have more faith. Similarly, there must be implicit trust in all matters financial between craftsperson and agent. Nothing sours a relationship faster than the suspicion of fiddling.

Try, wherever possible, to avoid agreeing to supply one agent exclusively, other than in strictly defined territories or with a specific range of goods. The possible exception would be if your agent agrees (in writing if you have any doubts) either to buy everything that you can produce or at the very least to guarantee you a minimum annual income. Failing that, allow a new agent a trial period of anything from a couple of months to a year, and let the results speak for themselves. If you are satisfied with the performance, so be it. If you do agree to a total exclusivity arrangement, be warned that you will not be able to break it without considerable difficulty.

You might, as a possible third alternative, choose to employ a **representative** to sell your work. A rep is basically a selling agent whose earnings usually come from a commission paid by the producer from sales rather than from a mark-up (paid by the customer) on the wholesale price as used by most other types of agent.

Once again, you will have to make a decision with regard to the usefulness and honesty of the person you choose as a rep. Give a good deal of thought to the question of commission rates. If you don't offer a high enough percentage, your representative will have no incentive to do well; if you pay too much, there will be no need for your reps to push for more sales than are absolutely necessary to earn them a decent living.

There are some instances when certain types of people are better suited to represent you than others. For example, if you are selling equipment to schools or playgroups, you will stand a far better chance if your representative or agent is someone with teaching experience – perhaps a schoolteacher who has left the profession to start a family, and now wishes to work on a part-time basis. Essentially your representative must be able to empathise with the customer; if that is the case, you will be more than half way to making a sale.

Always keep an eye on the sales performance of the agents who work on your behalf, and pay heed to what they report back from the customers with regard to what is selling successfully and what is not.

I would also recommend that you pay your representative the percentage commission from a sale only *after* the customer has paid you. It is not unknown for unscrupulous representatives to write out fictitious orders in order to gain commission.

21
Getting Paid

It is quite horrifying how many craftspeople are unaware of the niceties of chiselling what is rightfully theirs out of people who owe them money.

Not all customers are amnesiac in the matter of outstanding bills; in fact, you will probably find that the occasional non-payers will stand out glaringly from the bulk of your regular customers. But at best, non-payers are a nuisance, and at worst they can put your whole livelihood at risk if you are owed too much at the wrong time (for example, when you have to pay your own suppliers).

As with all things, there are certain basic absolutes in running a small business, and in this case it is that you provide either goods or services for which you will receive payment from whomever you supply. You will soon find that in the esoteric craft world it is hard enough to put a commercial value on your skills and harder still to be a 'tradesman' with a potential customer who appreciates your work for its artistic merit. Whilst I would not wish to promote complete hard-headed professionalism, I would like to encourage a clearer understanding of your goal which, apart from creating well-made and beautiful crafts, is to earn a living from your skills, and also perhaps to feed your family.

CASH IN HAND

Perhaps the easiest method of transaction is by exchanging your product for cash. If this cash should then disappear into your pocket, never to be seen again, there is every likelihood that you will disappear in like manner should the kindly men from HM

Inspectorate of Taxes ever disturb you in your activities. I cannot argue strongly enough against running a business in this manner, because, apart from the obvious illegality, unless you are extremely bright at financial wizardry (like making money disappear), you are almost bound to come unstuck sooner or later, probably sooner. And let's face it, if you are that bright in matters financial, what are you doing wasting your talents making craft items? So if you are paid in cash, please resist all temptation and try to keep a record of it.

CHEQUE

Probably the most common method of payment is by bank cheque, and provided you follow the guidelines for ascertaining that a cheque is made out correctly, you should be assured of being paid.

The basic rules when you are offered a cheque are to ensure that the date is entered correctly; the payee's name (your name in this instance) is correct; the amount in words agrees with the amount in figures, not to mention that the amount tallies with your invoice; and lastly that the cheque is properly signed. If the cheque is made out for £50 or less, you should check the signature against the customer's bank card and write the card number on the back of the cheque (make sure that the card is valid). By doing this you will guarantee payment by the bank should the customer have insufficient funds in the account. Don't waste your time asking to see a driver's licence; the only thing it will indicate is that the customer is allowed to drive. You are not required to ask for the customer's address on the back of a cheque, and they are perfectly within their rights to refuse to do so if they have already supplied their bank card number. However, if you want a record of the customer's address for any reason (perhaps you want to build up your own mailing list for publicity purposes), you could always ask for it to be written on the invoice.

TRAVELLER'S CHEQUE

When you are offered traveller's cheques, you must first ascertain whether they are in US dollars or sterling (you will rarely be given any other currency). If they are in sterling, you must ensure that your customers countersign the cheques in your presence, then compare the two signatures on each cheque with that on their passport (or other official identification document). The traveller's cheque should also be dated in your presence. Some shops insist that customers write their British address, albeit temporary, on the back of a cheque, in the hope that it will deter possible fraud.

Because of the amount of fraud involving traveller's cheques, you must protect yourself by being extremely vigilant when a customer offers them to you. The majority of transactions where traveller's cheques are used as payment are unquestionably above board, but if you are uncertain or suspicious you should ask your customers if they would change the cheques at a bank and pay you in cash. If the customer is bona fide and you are polite, they will usually agree to your request, and if not, then at worst you have lost a sale and at best you have avoided being swindled.

With regard to foreign currency travellers' cheques, you must telephone your bank to find out what the correct current rate is, allowing for bank charges.

FOREIGN CURRENCY

Where possible, try to avoid being paid in foreign currency. You will almost invariably come off the worst of the deal after you have coped with fluctuations in the exchange rates and bank commission charges. On no account quote the rates that are published in the newspapers or are displayed in banks because they do not take into account commission rates, which can be anything from £3 to £6 per transaction or more depending on the amount involved. This is why there is an unofficial rate of exchange called the 'hotel' rate which is far less favourable to the tourist, but from your point of view provides a safety margin against your losing your profits due to an unforeseen hiccup on the world money markets.

Should you decide to accept foreign currency on a regular basis, you will soon learn at what point above the daily bank rates to pitch your own personal 'hotel' rate in order to safeguard your prices against fluctuation. However, to be going on with, you should consider at least an eight per cent exchange differential in your favour.

If you develop regular export business, you might consider pricing your goods in foreign currency, which will certainly simplify matters for both you and your customers.

PLASTIC CARDS

More and more craftspeople are accepting 'plastic money'. It is not uncommon nowadays for the various cards to be accepted by market stallholders as well as by the more established shopkeepers. In the main, plastic cards divide into two categories: credit cards and charge cards. Credit cards allow the cardholder extended credit within an agreed personal limit, insofar as the amount owed may be paid back to the card company over a period of a few months. The two major credit card companies, and probably the only ones you will ever have to deal with, are Access (sometimes known as Mastercard or Eurocard) and Visa.

Charge cards differ from credit cards in that, whereas there is no credit-limit for the cardholder, the total amount owed must be paid immediately and in full each month. The two major international charge cards are American Express and Diner's Club. For the craftsperson whose business depends on selling to tourists, or if you are selling fairly expensive goods, the benefits of accepting cards are obvious; above all, they enable your customers to pay you with the least possible inconvenience to themselves. Apart from that, you may decide to use the mail- or telephone-order facility offered by the various card companies, thereby affording you speedy payment without having to wait for cheques that are delayed in the post or, in the case of exports, having to put up with the vagaries of the foreign exchange market.

Should you be interested in any of the schemes on offer, the relevant company will be more than happy to send along a representative to discuss its terms with you.

The cost to you when you accept plastic money is that the card company charge you a percentage of the business that you transact with its card scheme. Whereas each retail outlet is said to be assessed on its individual merits, the average service charge is generally about five per cent of the card transaction. At the moment Access and Visa charge retail outlets a once-only joining fee, whereas American Express do not.

Regardless which, if any, cards you accept – most retailers who accept cards at all take all of the major cards – the main benefit of the so-called cashless revolution is the sheer convenience to all concerned. After a while, if you find that your sales have markedly improved due to your accepting cards, so much the better. If you find that there is no noticeable change, or at least insufficient to justify the service charge, then, subject to your agreement with the card company, you should be able to opt out of the scheme.

INVOICE

An invoice is not a receipt, nor necessarily a demand for payment, but merely a record of a credit sale transaction between you and your customer. However, in most cases it is used in the form of 'payment against invoice' which essentially makes it a demand for payment for goods or services rendered to be settled within the specified time that you have agreed is to be your 'credit period'.

Assuming you are a sole trader and not registered for VAT, you can enter more or less whatever details you like on an invoice. Have a look at invoices that have been sent to you, and you will see that the information supplied will be broadly as follows:

1 Name of supplier	7 Quantity of goods
2 Name of customer	8 Unit price of goods
3 Invoice number	9 Sub-total of goods
4 Invoice date	10 Total
5 Customer's order number/	11 Discount
reference number	12 Total amount of invoice
6 Description of goods	

This really is the minimum amount of information that you should have on your invoice for it to be of any use to you as a record of a sale or a demand for payment (see Fig 6).

TERMS & CONDITIONS OF SALE

You would be well-advised to set out in a totally unambiguous way your terms and conditions of sale. In this way you will protect your interests and avoid any misunderstandings. In order that the customer is made fully aware of your terms you may choose to display them in your catalogue, on your order form or on the reverse side of your invoice. As a bare minimum your Terms and Conditions should include the following details: Terms of Payment; Minimum Quantity; Claims for Shortages & Damages; Title to Goods. An example is as follows:

TRADING TERMS & CONDITIONS

Payment: 30 days from date of invoice.
Minimum Order: For orders under £50 a £5.00 handling fee will be applied.
Claims: Shortages or damaged goods should be advised to us within 3 days of delivery.
Ownership of Goods: Goods remain the sole and absolute property of the Company until such time as the intending purchaser shall have paid the Company the agreed price.

E & O E

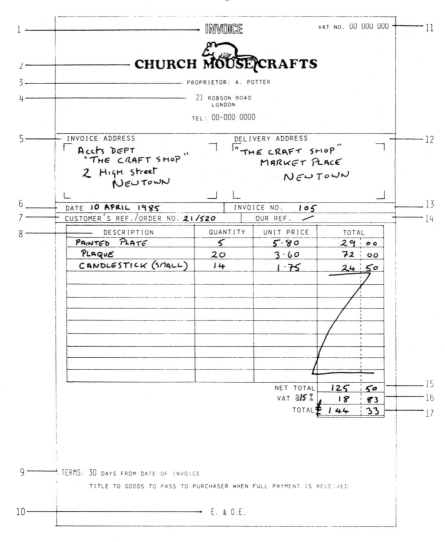

INVOICE

VAT NO. 00 000 000 — 11

CHURCH MOUSE CRAFTS

PROPRIETOR: A. POTTER

21 ROBSON ROAD
LONDON

TEL: 00-000 0000

INVOICE ADDRESS	DELIVERY ADDRESS
Accts DEPT "THE CRAFT SHOP" 2 HIGH Street NEWTOWN	"THE CRAFT SHOP" MARKET PLACE NEWTOWN

DATE **10 APRIL 1985** | INVOICE NO. **105**
CUSTOMER'S REF./ORDER NO. **21/520** | OUR REF.

DESCRIPTION	QUANTITY	UNIT PRICE	TOTAL	
PAINTED PLATE	5	5·80	29	00
PLAQUE	20	3·60	72	00
CANDLESTICK (small)	14	1·75	24	50
		NET TOTAL	125	50
		VAT @15%	18	83
		TOTAL £	144	33

TERMS: 30 DAYS FROM DATE OF INVOICE

TITLE TO GOODS TO PASS TO PURCHASER WHEN FULL PAYMENT IS RECEIVED

E. & O.E.

Fig 6 A typical invoice for a VAT-registered sole trader

Fig 6
1 Description of the form
2 Your business name and logo
3 Sole trader's name
4 Business address
5 Where to send invoice
6 Date of invoice and tax-point
7 Customer's reference or order number
8 Itemised breakdown of quantity and value of goods being invoiced
9 Your trading terms re payment etc
10 'Errors and omissions excepted' a catch-all clause in the event of errors in drawing up the invoice
11 VAT registration number (if registered)
12 Where to send goods
13 The invoice number
14 Your reference number
15 Sub-total of goods value, excluding VAT (or maybe discount if offered)
16 VAT value of goods
17 Grand total of invoiced goods

Unfortunately it is not enough to assume that everybody acts in good faith. Use your discretion and commonsense to tailor trading terms to suit your own particular business.

A **pro forma invoice** is an invoice as described above, sent by you to your customer for payment *before* the goods are despatched. This method of invoicing is usually employed for a customer with whom you have not previously dealt, and thus minimises your risk of extending credit by ensuring that you get paid up front.

A **statement** (see Fig 7) is basically a demand for payment. The normal period of credit in Britain is thirty days; in France it is often sixty days, and in the USA ninety days credit is not uncommon. Occasionally you can arrange your own period of credit with your customers, but it is in your own interest to do so beforehand to avoid any misunderstandings.

Assuming that your customer is in Britain, you would normally send your statement thirty days after the invoice date. If you have still not been paid thirty days after that, if the statements do not produce the desired effect (you getting paid),

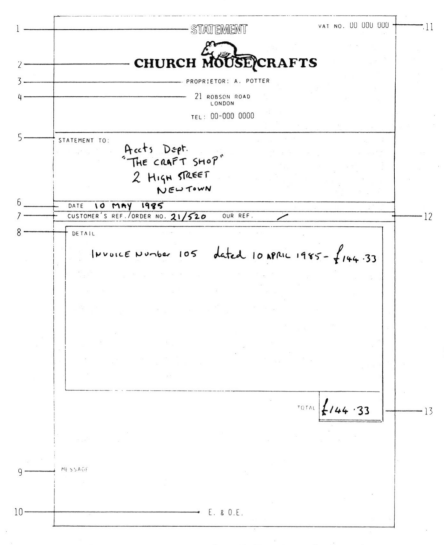

Fig 7 A typical statement for a VAT-registered sole trader

Fig 7
 1 Description of the form
 2 Your business name and logo
 3 Sole trader's name
 4 Business address
 5 Customer's name and address
 6 Date of statement
 7 Customer's reference or order number
 8 Itemised details of statement
 9 Additional message if required
10 'Errors and omissions excepted' a catch-all clause in the event of errors in drawing up the statement
11 VAT registration number (if registered)
12 Your reference
13 Grand total of monies owed

---

don't be shy about telephoning your customers and *politely* reminding them that they owe you some money. In fairness to them, if they are in business too, what may be a dramatic debt to you may have been completely forgotten by them in the general hurly-burly of their life.

Should you have to telephone any late payers (or, in the arcane language of accountants, 'aged debtors'), here is a list of the Top 20 best excuses for non-payment of outstanding invoices.

20 GOOD REASONS WHY YOU ARE BROKE

1 'It's in the post.' (It's so corny, it might even be true.)
2 'We posted it last week, but they collect the post round here at infrequent intervals.'
3 'According to our records, we paid last month.' (You prove otherwise.)
4 'Good Lord, is it sixty days already? I'll get onto it right away.'
5 'We're waiting for a new chequebook.'
6 'Our finance director is on holiday. We'll send you a cheque as soon as he/she returns.'

7 'Our finance director has a broken wrist and can't sign any cheques.'

8 'Our finance director has just died.'

9 'I'm sorry. Did we forget to sign the cheque?'

10 'I'm sorry. Did we forget to date the cheque?'

11 'I'm sorry. Did we forget to put a cheque in the envelope?'

12 'I'm sorry. Did we send you the wrong cheque?'

13 'I'm sorry. We sent you a cheque on our No 2 account, when all payments have to be made on our No 1 account.'

14 'Our books are with our accountant – as soon as he is finished with them . . .' etc.

15 'I should love to send you a cheque, but we need two signatures, and the other signatory is in Birmingham [or John 'o' Groats] at a trade fair.'

16 'We can't find your invoice anywhere. Could you please send us a copy?'

17 'We can't find a record of your invoice in our computer.' (Whether or not there actually is a computer.)

18 'Our computer keeps rejecting your invoice.' (To be rejected is bad enough, but by a computer!)

19 'Sorry, my son has flushed all our files down the loo and we are in a terrible state . . .'

20 'The office temp has put all this month's paperwork in the shredder.'

All of the above are ploys commonly used by customers who, whilst not unwilling to pay you (heaven forfend!), simply wish to extend their credit at your expense. The more inventive of your customers may use any of the above excuses with the addition of fire, flood or act of God. However it is much better to hear a well-honed excuse than the tone of a disconnected telephone number or even worse a hollow laugh when you ask to speak to the accounts department.

Finally you should always remember that, however embarrassed you may be about asking for payment, *you are only asking for what is yours.*

IV
GETTING THERE,
STAYING THERE

22
Staying Afloat

I apologise for this chapter being like the spectre at the feast, but I would be failing in my task if I pretended that everything will be 'sweetness and light', with no problems to disturb you. You will soon discover that being your own boss presents you with a continuous series of crises and challenges. We all make mistakes, some more than others, so don't allow yourself to think you are the only person in the world who has ever trusted a crook or lost money on a sale. Consider setbacks such as these as lessons learned, and try not to repeat them in the future.

The secret of survival will depend largely on your ability to keep problems within manageable limits. Problems are usually closely connected with money, or the lack of it, either as cause or effect. For this reason, keep your cashflow and budget under constant scrutiny. You will find it much easier to solve problems whilst they are tolerably controllable, rather than allow them to grow into a threat to the survival of your business.

Should a problem occur that you feel it is beyond your capabilities to solve, you must go and seek advice from a reliable source. Difficult as it may be to swallow your pride, no one will think any the less of you for appreciating your own limitations. If it looks as though you are heading for a financial crisis, make an appointment to discuss the situation with your bank manager, accountant or other financial adviser. You will find that banks will be more sympathetic towards you and your business if you take the trouble to keep them advised of your progress or lack of it. Your bank will also be able to offer you constructive advice and practical help if the manager is aware of your situation at an early enough stage. By this I am not suggesting that you should be on the phone to your bank manager or accountant every minute of every day, but simply that you should try to take a detached view of your affairs from time to time and, most important of all, not ignore bad news.

The best way to avert disaster is to structure your business in such a way that problems can be isolated, so that the failure of one range of products does not jeopardise the rest.

Should things go horribly wrong, which can occur, forget about the ethics of 'going down with the ship'. There are times when it is far wiser to be a rat than a captain. Accept the fact that you will have to cut your losses; by so doing you will come out of the affair with your pride a bit dented but otherwise intact. And if the worst comes to pass and your business fails – so be it. You can always make a come-back, and you can at least console yourself with the knowledge that you gave it a damn good try.

If at all possible – and I know that sometimes one has to take risks – don't over-extend yourself either financially or productively. Always try to keep something in reserve. You may never need it, but it will be reassuring for you to know it is there. Should you ever need to realise some capital to put into your venture, I cannot argue strongly enough against mortgaging or re-mortgaging your home: if your business fails for whatever reason, you stand to lose everything you possess. Similarly, you should think very carefully about giving a personal guarantee for any loan or commitment, because even if you are trading as a limited company you could lose everything if the business is in difficulties. I cannot believe that anything is worth literally 'going for broke'.

If you feel that a risk is worth taking, think it through carefully. To the best of your abilities try to evaluate the bottom line. In other words, is there going to be any percentage in it for you? After all, you should never forget that when it comes to the crunch you are the most important person to consider.

What I am trying to establish is that you must protect your own interests, because nobody else is going to be sufficiently interested to do so for you.

23
National Craft Organisations

Craftspeople are notorious for being loners. Nevertheless, by joining an organisation dedicated to promoting your particular craft you will stand a much better chance of establishing yourself in the market-place. The crafts world is very small, and word will soon get out about a new talent, if you give it a chance.

The only truly common factor I have found between all the craft guilds and societies is the immense enthusiasm members have for their particular craft. Every organisation has its own aims and criteria for membership: some are more interested in the technical practicalities; others offer their members a social life, with talks and visits related to their craft.

I know, from my own experience, that joining a guild at the time I actively started to make and sell toys gave me the opportunity to meet established craftspeople in my field. I could see what standards of expertise they worked to, and slowly I began to learn by their example. For me the best thing about being a member of a craft organisation is the knowledge that one is not completely isolated, because if you work on your own it is terribly easy to become a hermit.

Most of the craft organisations formed over the past thirty or forty years have come about as a result of a few concerned craftspeople who got together to improve the overall quality and protect the integrity of their craft against the dross that was being sold at that time. Generally the natural direction of a craft organisation is steadily to promote and improve the quality of the craft that it represents, whilst at the same time educating the public to appreciate and buy well-made and well-designed products.

In the end, you may decide not to bother about joining a national or regional craft body, but before you make that decision, see what they have to offer.

The following list of national craft organisations is by no means complete. However, I hope it will give you some idea of what is available and will point you in the right direction, should you decide to join one. You will notice that I have not included the telephone numbers of the associations and guilds: they tend to change annually with the newly elected officers.

Art Workers Guild, 6 Queen Square, London WC1N 3AR

Basketmakers Association, Millfield Cottage, Little Hadham, Ware, Herts

Worshipful Company of Blacksmiths, 41 Tabernacle Street, London EC2

British Artist Blacksmiths Association, c/o Brontë Cottage, Barley Mow Hill, Arford, Headley, Bordon, Hants

Society of Designer Bookbinders, 6 Queen Square, London WC1N 3AR

Master Carvers Association, Stanhope Lodge, Arundel Road, Clapham, Worthing, Sussex NB13 3UA

Institute of Ceramics, Federation House, Stoke-on-Trent, Staffs ST4 2RY

The British Doll Artists Association, 67 Victoria Drive, Bognor Regis, Sussex

Artist Enamellers, 129 Chestnut Grove, London SW12 8JH

Guild of Craft Enamellers, Renarden, Lyth Hill, Shrewsbury, Salop SY3 0BS

Egg Crafters Guild of Great Britain, The Studio, 7 Hylton Terrace, North Shields, Tyne & Wear NE29 0EE

Embroiderers Guild, Apartment 41A, Hampton Court Palace, East Molsey, Surrey KT8 9AU

The Worshipful Company of Farriers, 3 Hamilton Road, Cockfosters, Barnet, Herts EN4 9EU

British Artists in Glass, 11 Brook Street, Stourbridge, W. Midlands

Guild of Glass Engravers, 19 Portland Place, London W1N 4BH
British Society of Master Glass Painters, 6 Queen Square, London WC1N 3AR
Institute of Architectural Ironmongers, 15 Soho Square, London W1V 5FB
The Knitting Craft Group, PO Box 6, Thirsk, N. Yorkshire
The Lace Guild, White House, Lowe Lane, Franche, Kidderminster, Worcs
The Lace Society, Lynwood, Startford Road, Oversley, Alcester, Warwickshire
Association of Designer Leatherworkers, 37 Silver Street, Tetbury, Glos GL8 8DI
Marquetry Society, 2A The Ridgeway, St Albans, Herts AL4 9AU
The College of Masons, 42 Magdalen Road, Wandsworth, London SW18 3NP
Early Music Instrument Makers Association, Little Critchmere, Manor Crescent, Haslemere, Surrey
Association of British Pewter Craftsmen, Heathcote Close, 136 Hagley Road, Edgbaston, Birmingham
Craftsman Potters Association, William Blake House, Marshall Street, London W1
The Quilters Guild, Clarendon, 56 Wilcot Road, Pewsey, Wilts SN9 5EL
The British Toymakers Guild, 240 The Broadway, Wimbledon, London SW19
Guild of Woodworkers, PO Box 35, Wolsey House, Wolsey Road, Hemel Hempstead, Herts HP2 4SS
Guild of Wrought Iron Craftsmen, The Forge, Commercial Road, Penryn, Cornwall

24
Ages and Stages

Everyone will tell you that there is never a good time to start up in business. If you allowed yourself to believe them, the arguments against your succeeding in business would be almost overwhelming. But so it was for everybody who has ever been in the same position that you now find yourself in, and there are a heck of a lot of successful companies that have survived.

If you have enough faith in yourself, combined with a smidgeon of caution and an inordinate amount of luck, you will stand a good chance of success.

Allow yourself to develop at your own pace, otherwise you will burn yourself out before you have managed to establish the natural potential of your business. It nearly always takes about three years before a small company is able to be truly profitable. This is due partly to the limited capital resources at its disposal but also because, as a rule, a small business will require at least that long to consolidate and co-ordinate its production capacity and capital resources to its market capabilities.

Regardless of how long you stay in business, you will have to contend with crises on an almost daily basis. A self-employed furniture-maker once described to me how he felt about the early days of his business. 'When I started out in business I knew all the answers, but not the questions,' he said. 'After five years, when I began to understand the questions, I found that I no longer knew the answers.'

In this chapter I have tried to point out the major milestones that you will almost certainly encounter on the way. I hope you have the good sense to regard the following list as a helpful map of the territory rather than a compulsory route through the minefield, because your survival will depend largely on your instinctive ability to cope with crises as and when they occur.

Before You Start

● Decide to set up on your own using skills or talents developed from a hobby, previous employment or education.

● Go to the various advisory bodies and organisations to obtain as much information as possible.

● Visit as many craft fairs, shows and markets as you can. Chat to established craftspeople.

● Talk to the bank (where you have your personal account) and let the manager know about your plans for the future. Ask for the manager's advice.

● Shop around and choose a suitable bank for your business account. (It can be the same branch as your personal account if you are happy with their terms and service.)

● Find workspace to suit your optimum requirements with regard to space and expense.

● Prepare draft cashflow forecasts and contact (or re-contact) your town hall or local development agency, to find out what they could do to assist you. Be prepared to accept their suggestions with regard to the presentation of your plans. No one will hold you responsible if you cannot live up to your forecasts; they are simply to show that you have given your scheme due consideration.

● By now you will be looking at the cost of tools and equipment. You should also be actively seeking out sources of supply for materials.

● You should have formed a good idea of what you want to make. (If not, you had better get a move on.) You have probably started to make samples to show potential customers.

● Contact an accountant and discuss the broad outlines of your proposed business venture. Listen carefully to what you are told with regard to book-keeping methods; it could save you a lot of money in the future.

● Contact a solicitor if you need to (regarding leasing property, agreeing partnership, arranging terms and conditions of loans, etc).

● Think about a trade name, and design a suitable logo. Prepare the artwork for your stationery requirements.

● Plan, plan, plan. The more planning you do before you start, the easier your first and subsequent years will be.

First Year

● By now you will have moved into your workspace and started to buy in equipment and materials. Spend two or three weeks arranging your workspace to suit your requirements. If you are renting property, it is customary to allow a settling-in period of a few weeks that is rent-free.

● Start production. Test your products either by selling to local shops or making appointments to see buyers in specialist shops or departments. Alternatively you could rent a stall at a craft market. Find the option you feel most comfortable with and give it a try. How you sell and whom you propose to sell to are entirely your own affair; what is good for you would probably not suit somebody else.

● Contact the press and try to get as much free publicity as possible – otherwise nobody will know of your existence.

● During your first year you will probably make a cash loss for the first couple of months, have a few months that just about break even and one or two months that will be terrific. Overall you will probably make a trading loss – nobody will expect you to make a net profit in your first year. In fact, your accountant will probably advise you to make a loss if you can, so that it can be offset against later years' profit liabilities.

Second Year

● By now you will have a fairly good idea of what it is all about.
● People will have passed conflicting opinions about your

work. The nice people will have bought from you, and the others will go off and annoy some other poor craftsperson.

● You will find that people are contacting you out of the blue. They will have a) read about you in the newspapers; b) seen your work at a friend's house; c) been told about your work.

● You will have noticed that you are able to produce more items per week than you could have made in a whole month last year.

● By now you should be able to tell which items sell and which do not. Rationalise your range, drop the non-sellers and introduce some new items into the range so that you keep it fresh whilst retaining the popular items.

● By the end of the second year you will have learned the distinction between turnover and profit. You will probably have achieved an impressive turnover, in terms of both unit sales and cash, but you will probably be left with little profit, if any at all. This is due partly to the first year's trading loss and partly to the fact that you will not yet have settled into a viable cashflow rhythm between expenditure and income.

NB: Unless you are careful, in your second year you will find that your book-keeping will be in a chaotic state. As a rule, an untidy workspace or shop means a busy one.

Third Year and Forever

● Your third year will be much like the second, except that you will probably be trading at an increased level and buying in greater quantities of materials (at lower average prices, I hope).

● You will probably be employing people on a part- or full-time basis to help you make or sell your product.

● By now your accountant should be able to detect the glimmer of a profit and you will be able to claim back any tax due because of your previous years' losses.

● Congratulations! If you have managed to hang in there for three years, there is no reason to suspect that you will not be able to keep going until you decide to quit.

A Glossary of Basic Business Terms

Account   A calculation; a statement of monies received or paid out; a record of financial transactions; a customer or client or a client's business affairs.

Accountant   See also Book-keeper and Chartered Accountant. Someone with a specialised knowledge of finance, commerce and book-keeping.

Agent   A person or company authorised by you to act on your behalf to take orders, buy, sell and represent you and your company.

Allowances   See also Discount. A stated amount of income allowed to be free of tax or to be deducted from taxable income by the tax-payer. An agreed reduction in price.

Assessment   In the absence of accurate figures, readings or audited accounts, the relevant authorities may assess your estimated debt.

Asset   A possession that has a monetary value that can be used to pay off debts.

Audit   An official examination of a company's accounts by an independent qualified person, in order to show that they represent a true record of that company's affairs at year-end.

Avoidance   Action taken to avoid having to pay tax unnecessarily whilst keeping strictly within the law.

Bailiff   An officer of the court empowered to enforce the court's decisions. He is authorised to seize property in order to obtain payment for debt.

Balance sheet   A statement showing the financial position of a business, usually at year end.

Bankrupt   To be unable to pay one's debts or meet one's commitments, and to have a court-appointed trustee administer one's affairs.

Black Economy   Goods or services that are sold for cash and not recorded, thus avoiding – or, strictly speaking, evading – tax.

Bodging   The art of improvisation. The term originates from the 'chair bodgers' of High Wycombe, itinerant craftsmen who specialised in the manufacture of legs and stretchers for the Windsor chair.

Book-keeper   See Accountant and Chartered Accountant. A person employed to keep (make records of and update) the accounts of a business.

Business Name   The name or title under which a company trades.

Cabbage   A term used predominantly in the clothing industry to describe surplus produce obtained by shrewd manipulation of materials.

Capital   Money or monetary value of assets.

Capital Expenditure   Money spent by a business on fixed assets or materials used in the manufacturing process.

Cashflow   Information about the financial performance in a budget forecast. The amount of cash made by a business within a specified time.

Chartered Accountant   See Book-keeper and Accountant. An accountant who is fully qualified to audit public company accounts. A member of one of the Institutes of Chartered Accountants. Chartered accountants are distinguished by the letters FCA or ACA (in Scotland CA) after their names.

Close (verb)   To finalise a deal.

COD   Cash On Delivery. A condition made by the supplier in which, by prior agreement, goods despatched by post or other means will be paid for by the buyer at time of delivery.

Collateral   Property or other article held as security against a loan.

Co-operative   A business or organisation owned and run by a group of persons or a society whose aim is to benefit the members.

Copyright   A legal right, usually belonging to a person who creates literary, artistic or musical work, preventing anyone from copying it without permission. The duration of copyright is generally the lifetime of the owner and fifty years after death.

Credit   A period of time a supplier gives to a customer to pay for goods supplied; payment received; a method of trading on trust allowing the customer to pay at a mutually agreed later date; to have disposable funds in the bank.

Credit Note   Acknowledgement of a cash or credit reversal due to invoice error or return of goods.

Creditor   See Preferential Creditor and Secured Creditor. A person or organisation to whom money is owed.

Day Book   A book in which are recorded all the day-to-day purchase and sale transactions of a business.

Debit   A payment out. The opposite of credit.

Debit Note   Similar to an invoice, but usually relates to charges extra to amounts already invoiced for goods. It is also used to adjust and correct errors in an invoice.

Debtor   A person who owes money.

Deposit   A sum of money given as part payment of the total price of goods purchased; money or equivalent left in a bank or similar institution as security or to bear interest.

Discount   See Allowance. A reduction from the list price, usually given for quantity, trade, cash settlement or early payment.

E&OE   Errors and Omissions Excepted. Printed on invoices, etc, it allows for mistakes to be amended at a later date.

Estimate   A statement of probable cost for goods and services that is liable to change.

Evasion   Non-payment of tax, using illegal means.

Financial year   An accounting period, usually one complete twelve month period though this need not be the case. It may not necessarily coincide either with the calendar year or with the tax year.

FOB   Free On Board. A term used in export. The seller's price includes all charges and risks up to the point when the goods are delivered on board the ship named by the buyer. In some cases FOB may apply to other forms of transport or intermediate addresses.

Freelance   A skilled person who does not work as an employee but is available to work for anyone who wishes to use his or her services in return for a fee.

Goodwill   An asset consisting of the good reputation of an established business. Hard to quantify, it is generally used when negotiating the sale or transfer of a business.

Grant   See Loan. An amount of money given to individuals or companies by an institution or agency to enable it to begin, expand or develop its business.

Gross   Total before deductions.

Homeworker   See Outworker. A person who sub-contracts or does piecework at their home for payment, on behalf of the producer.

Insolvency   A situation in which a person or business is not able to meet financial obligations, although the debts may be paid if the assets of the person or business are realised (sold).

Interest   Money paid for the use or loan of capital, either at previously agreed rates or at an agreed percentage of the banks' minimum lending rate.

Job Off   To get rid of slow-selling or old stock by selling cheaply.

Job Out   To give out work to a number of contractors.

Lease   An agreement in writing in which one person gives another the right to use land or goods for a fixed period in return for either a single sum of money (premium) or a series of regular payments (rent) or a combination of both.

Leaseback   A method of realising an asset whilst retaining its use.

The owner sells his or her property on condition that it can be leased back at an agreed rent for a fixed period.

Liability   Debts of all kinds; to be bound by law to settle a debt or to make good loss or damage.

Licence   A formal permit. Sometimes used for short or indeterminate use of premises as an alternative to a lease.

Liquid Asset   Asset which can be turned into cash at short notice.

Liquidation   The legal process of closing down a bankrupt company and realising its assets to pay the debts.

Liquidity   The extent of the cash assets of a business. Including other assets that can be realised for cash.

Loan   See Grant. Amount of money loaned to an individual or company to be repaid at an agreed date and usually at an agreed rate of interest.

Long Firm   A company that is formed for the specific purpose of obtaining goods on credit with the intention of never paying for them.

Mailshot   A concentrated campaign of postal advertising.

Merchantable Quality   Goods of a sufficient quality to satisfy the purposes for which they were intended. Goods fit for sale.

Net, also Nett   Total after deductions.

Office of Fair Trading   A central body responsible for laws protecting the rights of the consumer. The local authority's Trading Standards Officers department is responsible for enforcing the legislation.

Order Book   A book in which orders to supply goods are recorded as soon as they are received.

Output   The value of all goods produced and/or services performed by a business.

Outworker   See Homeworker and Sub-contractor.

Overdraft   A previously agreed amount that a bank loans to a person or business. An overdraft may be called in by the lender at any time should it so wish.

Overhead   Cost that does not vary with the rate of production (eg rent).

P & P   Post and Packing. The amount charged on an invoice to cover the cost of despatch.

Patent   A legal protection to safeguard the exclusivity of manufacture of a new product or invention. The life of a patent is sixteen years but this can be extended by five or ten years in certain cases.

Piracy   A polite description for the unauthorised manufacture of someone else's original work.

Preferential Creditor   See Creditor. A creditor who, by law, is paid first from the distribution of assets of a bankrupt.

Pro Forma   An invoice sent to a customer, usually a first-time buyer, who has to pay for the goods before they are sent.

Public Liability   An insurance policy that protects a professional or business person against claims made by the public for damages allegedly caused by the goods or services supplied.

Quality Control   A system for checking the quality of materials and finished products so that a standard quality is maintained.

Quotation   See Estimate. A statement of the current price and conditions that a supplier of goods or services is offering.

Receipt   A written acknowledgement that money due has been paid or that goods have been received.

Reference   Person or firm named by a customer requesting credit, from whom the supplier can obtain information about the customer's business reputation.

Registered Office   An office that every company must have by law, whose full address is formally registered with the Registrar of Companies.

Royalties   Payment calculated on a percentage of sales or business transacted.

Schedule D   The Inland Revenue schedule which defines the tax allowances for the self-employed.

Secured Creditor   See Creditor. A person holding a mortgage or lien on some or all of the property of a debtor as security for the debt.

Self-Employed   A person working on his or her own, either as a freelance or in their own business. Subject to Schedule D tax.

Statement   A document sent regularly (monthly) by a seller to a credit buyer noting details of invoices issued and payments received. A statement is a demand for payment of outstanding debts.

Stock   Finished goods, goods in production and raw materials, all of which are considered part of the capital resources of a business.

Stock Taking   The practice of compiling an inventory of every asset held in stock, usually at the end of the financial year, in order to make an accurate stock evaluation.

Stock Control   System of checking the stock of goods and materials held by a business, providing a clear appreciation of the quantity and distribution.

Sub-contractor   A person or business who agrees to provide materials or services for another party to perform another contract.

Trade Description   A description of goods or services for the purpose of attracting buyers. It is an offence to make a false or misleading description of goods offered for sale.

Trade Discount   A discount allowed by a manufacturer or wholesaler to a retailer.

Trade Price   The price paid by a retailer to a wholesaler.

VAT   Value Added Tax. A tax that is levied on sales at all stages of production.

Working Capital   The assets and cash needed by a business to keep trading.

Bibliography

*free publication

Barret, E. and Fogden, L. *Guide to Good Craft Suppliers* (Argus Books Ltd)
Export Handbook (HMSO)
Hints to Exporters, a series of booklets (BOTB)*
Macara, Daphne, Ed., *Croner's Reference Book for the Self Employed & Smaller Business* (Croner Publications Ltd)
Running a Workshop (Crafts Council)
Schumacher, E. F. *Small is Beautiful* (Abacus 1974)
Small Firms Service publications, a series of booklets by various authors (Department of Trade & Industry)*
Starting in Business (The Board of the Inland Revenue)*
St John Price, A. *Buying a Shop* (Kogan Page)
Swanson, C., Phillips, P., Barrow, B. *Co-operating for Work* (COIC)
Why SOBs Succeed and Nice Guys Fail in a Small Business (Financial Managements Assoc Inc)

Acknowledgements

I would like to thank the following for their help in the preparation of this book: Peter Checksfield, who provided the illustrations; the numerous craftspeople who shared their tales of woe with me; my word-processor, without which I would still be typing the first draft.

My thanks also to the British Toymakers Guild for the fellowship and support it has given me all the time I have been pursuing my craft; my suppliers, who give me credit; my customers, who keep me in business; and all the super people I have met since becoming a self-employed jobbing toymaker.

Index

Index

Newspapers, 82, 104, 106, 107, 109, 134

One-offs, 76, 82
Outworkers, 58, 59, 71, 138
Overdrafts, 13, 15, 32, 138
Overheads, 70, 76, 77, 79, 93, 94, 138

Part-time employees, 59, 60, 71, 74, 113
Partners, partnership, 20–22, 23, 34, 69
Patents, 51, 138
    Patent Office, 51
PAYE, 60, 68, 71
Personal guarantee, 127
Photographs, publicity, 107, 109
Post, 31, 90–1, 103
Postpacks, 103
Premises, 29, 31, 38–44
Presentation, 15, 33–4, 52, 55
Press, 92
    see also Newspapers
Press release, 107, *108*
Pricing, 58, 62, 76–80, 88, 94, 98, 117
Printing, 76, 78, 93
PRO, 106
Pro-forma invoice, 102, 121, 139
Profits, 20, 21, 69, 76, 78, 79, 131, 134
Publicity, 92, 104, 115
Public liability, 30–1, 103, 139
Purchases, 33, 41, 63, 72, 73, 89

Quality control, 58, 139

Radio, 82, 107, 109
Rates, 33, 39, 40, 48, 70, 77
References, 64, 139
Registrar of Companies, 26, 27
Registry of Business Names, 25
Rent, 14, 33, 36, 39, 41, 48, 70, 74, 77, 94
Retail, 88, 89, 90

Safety at Work Act 1974, 42
Sale or return, 90

Scottish Development Agency, 35, 39, 50, 51
Securicor, 91
Shop, 57, 82, 83, 84–5, 88, 89, 90, 94
SITPRO, 103
Small Business Advice Centre, 18
Small Firms Service, 27, 39, 52, 68
Sole trader, 19–20, 23, 25, 69
Solicitor, 13, 18, 19, 21, 23, 34, 56, 133
Staff, *see* Employees
Statements, 121–3, *122*, 139
Stationary, 26, 44, 133
Statutory rights, 65
Stock, 30, 41, 58, 63, 86, 93, 94, 139
Sub-contractors, 57, 74, 139
Suppliers, 14, 15, 40, 57, 62–7, 73, 114

Tax, 17, 22, 68–72
    Assessment, 70
    Capital gains, 70
    Corporation, 69
    Income, 69–70
    Inspector of Taxes, 68, 115
    Returns, 18, 68, 70
    Schedule 'D', 69, 139
    Tax office, 60
    VAT, 68, 71–2, 118, 140
Teaching, 74
Television, 106, 107
Terms & conditions of sale, 119
Title to goods, 119
Top Drawer, trade fair, 100
Track record, 16, 20, 32–3, 64
Trade prices, 63, 76, 87, 88, 140
Trade unions, 61

Unfair dismissal, 61
URBED, 52
USA, 31, 101, 121

VAT, *see* Tax
Vehicle, 31, 77
Visa, 117–18

Wages, 14, 30, 69
Welsh Development Agency, 39, 52
Wholesalers, 63, 76, 88

144